CHICAGO CUBS FACTS & TRIVIA

by

Wayne Mausser

The E. B. Houchin Company
1996

South Bend, Indiana

The E. B. Houchin Company
23700 Marquette Blvd. A-8
South Bend, Indiana 46628

Copyright 1996 by the Publisher on behalf of the Author

All rights reserved, which include the right
to reproduce this book or any portions thereof
in any form whatsoever without prior written consent
from the publisher.

ISBN: 0-938313-14-2

First Edition First Printing: March 1996

Cover Art by Peggy Eagan

Photos and Photos of Trading Cards from Author's Private Collection

Printed in USA

TABLE OF CONTENTS

1
EARLY CUBS   **9**
History and 50 questions about the Cubs of the 1870s.

2
ADRIAN "CAP" ANSON: THE FIRST STAR   **15**
Brief biography and 20 questions about the first superstar in Cubs history.

3
OTHER EARLY STARS   **19**
Brief sketches of some of the other early stars of the Cubs. Ed Williamson, 10 questions; King Kelly, 10 questions; Bill Hutchison, 10 questions; Clark Griffith, 10 questions; Jimmy Ryan, 15 questions; Fred Pfeffer, 11 questions; Tommy Burns, 10 questions; and 100 other questions about that era.

4
THE EARLY YEARS OF THE 20TH CENTURY   **37**
Brief history of the era and sketches of some of the stars. Frank Chance, 12 questions; Johnny Kling, 11 questions; Johnny Evers, 10 questions; Joe Tinker, 11 questions; Mordecai Brown, 14 questions; Frank Schulte, 16 questions; Heinie Zimmerman, 10 questions; and 106 more questions about that era.

5
WRIGLEY TAKES OVER   **59**
Brief history of the 'teens and early '20s and sketches of some players. Grover Alexander, 12 questions; Bill Killefer, 10 questions; Hack Miller, 10 questions; Hippo Vaughn, 15 questions; Fred Mitchell, 10 questions; and 86 more questions

about that era.

6
THE JOE MCCARTHY ERA — 75
Brief history of the team and sketch of Joe McCarthy with 10 questions and sketches of other stars of the period. Rogers Hornsby, 10 questions; Hack Wilson, 10 questions; and 45 more questions covering McCarthy's tneure as manager of the Cubs.

7
REBUILDING AND SUCCESS — 85
Brief history of the period and sketches of some star players. Gabby Hartnett, 10 questions; Charlie Grimm, 10 questions; Billy Herman, 10 questions; and 42 more questions about the Cubs of the '30s.

8
THE WAR-TIME CUBS — 95
Brief history of the Cubs during World War II and sketches of some representative players. Stan Hack, 10 questions; Phil Cavarretta, 10 questions; Claude Passeau, 10 questions; and 50 more questions about the Cubs during WW II.

9
THE TOUGH YEARS — 105
Brief history about the years between WW II and the coming of Ernie Banks and sketches of a few players of the period. Bob Rush, 5 questions; Hank Sauer, 10 questions; Ralph Kiner, 5 questions; and 40 more questions about the other players of the time.

10
THE MAKING OF A SLUGGER — 113
The arrival of Ernie Banks and sketches of Banks with 25 questions and Gene Baker with 5 questions, and 43 more questions about the late '50s.

Chicago Cubs Facts & Trivia

11
THE GREAT EXPERIMENT   **121**
    The College of Coaches and a sketch of Ken Hubbs with 10 questions and 30 more questions about the era.

12
THE LIP AT THE HELM   **127**
    Brief history of Leo Duroucher's tenure as Cubs manager, a sketch of Duroucher, and sketches of several stars of the time. Ron Santo, 10 questions; Billy Williams, 10 questions; Don Kessinger, 10 questions; Glenn Beckert, 10 questions; Ferguson Jenkins, 10 questions; and 31 more questions about that time.

13
TOUGH TIMES   **139**
    Brief history of the 1970s and sketches of a few good men. Rick Monday, 5 questions; Bill Madlock, 5 questions; Rick Reuschel, 5 questions; and 50 more questions about the era.

14
CLOSE BUT NO CIGAR: FUTILITY LIVES!   **147**
    Brief history of the Dallas Green era to the present and sketches of several players of the time. Keith Moreland, 5 questions; Gary Matthews, 5 questions; Rick Sutcliffe, 5 questions; Andre Dawson, 5 questions; Mark Grace, 5 questions; Ryne Sandberg, 11 questions; and 50 more questions about that period of time.

THE ANSWERS   **161**

ABOUT THE AUTHOR   **181**

READ MORE ABOUT THE CUBS   **183**

Wayne Mausser

*To Linda,
Thanks for all your patience,
With Love*

CHICAGO CUBS FACTS & TRIVIA

1
EARLY CUBS

It seems as if everyone is a Cubs fan at one time or another. You learn to anticipate and then suffer as they find a way to stumble down the home stretch. But no matter how good or how bad the team is, there's always plenty of excitement and drama to last through another off season and make you long for spring training and a brand new opening day. Oh, what a team and what a history!

As for their history, the Cubs were originally known as the Chicago White Stockings and were founded October 12, 1869. The reason for the nickname is obvious. The White Stockings wore white hose.

Chicago was competitive right away, winning the coveted "whip-flag" in 1870, then in 1871, finishing 2nd in the newly created National Association. Interestingly, they had to play their last three games on the road because their baseball park was destroyed in the Great Chicago Fire. The White Stockings lost all three.

After that great beginning, the White Stockings played semi-pro in 1872 and 1873, renting their field to other pro teams to raise money so they could re-enter the National Association in 1874. The club did not fare very well that year. Then in June of 1875, the White Stockings came under the control of William Hulbert, a Chicago businessman, who later became majority owner. With the help of Albert G. Spalding, a pitcher Hulbert signed away from Boston, the National League constitution and by-laws were drafted in 1875 and the

National League was created in 1876. Besides Spalding, who was named manager, Hulbert had also picked up infielder Adrian "Cap" Anson and outfielder Bob "The Magnet" Addy from the Athletic Club of Philadelphia, second baseman Ross Barnes, first baseman Cal McVey, and catcher James White, all three from Boston. These five signees and Spalding, plus a handful of holdovers from the previous Chicago team, resulted in the White Stockings winning the first National League pennant in 1876.

After Spalding retired from playing a few years later to attend to his sporting goods business, Anson was appointed manager in 1879. The White Stockings went on to win pennants in 1880, 1881, 1882, 1885, and 1886. From 1887 thru 1891, Chicago finished 2nd three times and 3rd twice. But by then, many of the stars had been traded. By 1898, Anson had been fired and despite a good showing that year, the team would continue to flounder as the century came to an end.

Trivia Questions

1. On what date in 1876 did the franchise play its first game?

2. Who won the game?

3. Who were the losers?

4. What was the score?

5. How many clubs were original charter members of the National League?

6. Where was William Hulbert born?

7. In what year was he born?

Chicago Cubs Facts & Trivia

8. How old was he when he died?

9. Where in Illinois was Albert Spalding born?

10. Where did Spalding begin his semi-professional baseball career?

11. What was the name of his first team?

12. How old was Spalding when he began is semi-pro career?

13. Spalding pitched with what club in the National Association from 1871 thru 1875?

14. During that five-year span, how many games did he win?

15. What were his most wins in a season?

16. In what year did that occur?

17. How many victories did Spalding have in his first year with Chicago?

18. How many games did he lose?

19. How many innings did he pitch?

20. How many shutouts did he have?

21. At that time, what was the pitching distance to home plate?

22. When Spalding didn't pitch, what position did he play?

23. In what year did Spalding retire as a player?

24. In what year did he take over as owner and president of the team?

25. *The Spalding Guide*, an annual baseball feature, was later taken over by what publication?

26. Who took over in 1878 as Chicago's field manager?

27. The team's first spring training was held where?

28. In what year?

29. Who was named the club president in 1892?

30. Who collected the franchise's first RBI?

31. What myth did *The Spalding Guide* perpetrate?

32. In what year was Spalding elected to the Hall of Fame?

33. On what date in 1876 was the team's home opener played?

34. Where was the location of the first stadium?

35. What was the score and who won?

36. What position did Ross Barnes play?

37. On May 2, 1876, Barnes accomplished what?

38. Barnes became the club's first batting champion. What was his average?

Chicago Cubs Facts & Trivia

39. After 1876, how many times did Barnes hit .300?

40. What position did Bob Ferguson play?

41. Ferguson received a nickname for being able to catch line drives. What was it?

42. What position did Abner Dalrymple play?

43. In 1884, Dalrymple became the first player in National League history to do what?

44. What was Dalrymple's lifetime batting average?

45. This pitcher won 29 games in 1878 and 30 in 1879. Who was he?

46. What was this pitcher's lifetime record?

47. What caused his career to come to an end?

48. Frank Flint played what position?

49. What was Flint's nickname?

50. What piece of equipment did he refuse to wear?

2
ADRIAN "CAP" ANSON: THE FIRST STAR

Adrian Constantine Anson was the glue that held the National League Chicago White Stockings together from the beginning of the franchise until very late in the 19th Century.

Anson was beckoned to Chicago from Philadelphia by Al Spalding, and in his first season with the White Stockings in 1876, he played third base and hit .343 to help Chicago win the league's first pennant. In 1879, he took over as captain (field manager in those days) and also began playing first base. Anson's team dominated the league until a near fatal illness sidelined him late in the season, causing his team to fold; but in 1880, Chicago won the pennant and set a record by winning 21 consecutive games, which was a record until the 1916 New York Giants also reeled off 21 in a row.

Besides managing, Anson was also the team's leading hitter, and he won four batting championships, drove in more than 100 runs seven times in an eight-year stretch, and scored more than 100 runs in six consecutive seasons. He had a keen eye and was never struck out more than 30 times in any season. Anson could dodge a pitch, too. During his 22 years with Chicago, he reportedly was never hit by a pitch!

For 19 seasons, Anson was player-manager of the White Stockings and ran the team with an iron hand, but opponents often referred to him as "Baby" Anson. On the one hand, he was considered to be a fair man, while on the other, he was the one man most responsible for African-Americans being barred from Major League Baseball until Jackie Robinson was brought up to the Brooklyn Dodgers by Branch Rickey in 1947.

In 1884, brothers Moses and Welday Walker were playing with Toledo of the American Association. Anson's team was scheduled to play Toledo in an exhibition game, but when Anson found out the Walkers were black, he demanded they be removed from the field. The Walkers were not ordered off the diamond, but a similar incident occurred with Newark of the International Association three years later, and this time, an African-American pitcher by the name of George Stovey, walked off the field after Anson protested. By 1900, professional baseball was totally segregated.

As Anson's playing career started to wind down in the 1890s, his relationship with the team's front office also began to deteriorate. In 1892, James A. Hart took over as club president, and as time went on, the relationship between the two men grew worse. The next few years were a blend of some mediocre but mostly dismal seasons, and on February 1, 1898, Anson was released as manager of the White Stockings. He later served briefly as skipper of the New York Giants, and after later forming his own semi pro-team, he was still playing first base at the ripe old age of 59!

Anson also owned a billiard hall and was elected Chicago city clerk as a Democrat in 1905. His political career was short as he was defeated in a re-election bid two years later.

After his death, Anson was elected to the Baseball Hall of Fame in 1939.

Trivia Questions

1. Where was Anson born?

2. When was he born?

3. Where did Anson attend college?

4. How many years did he go there?

5. Anson first played professionally with what team in the National Association?

6. What was his highest single season batting average?

7. In what year did that occur?

8. How many pennants did Anson win as a manager with Chicago?

9. What was his lifetime batting average?

10. On October 3, 1897, he became the oldest player to do what?

11. When did he record his 3,000th hit?

12. How many hits did he have in his career?

13. How many home runs did he hit?

14. How many runs did he score?

15. How many RBIs did he have?

16. As manager of Chicago, how many games did he win?

17. How many games did he lose?

18. What was Anson's average in his final big league season?

19. Where did Chicago finish in his last season as manager?

20. When did Anson die?

3
OTHER EARLY STARS

Cap Anson was not the only star in Chicago during the 19th Century. There were many others who need to be mentioned, so here goes.

Ed Williamson

Ed Williamson was one of the team's first sluggers. The right-handed hitting third baseman made the most of a very short right field fence and a temporary change in the rules to smash a record 27 home runs in 1884. Prior to that, any ball hit over that portion of the fence was an automatic double.

But in 1884, the batter was given a home run and the balls started flying out of Lake Front Park. Williamson became the first player in history to hit three home runs in a single game, in the second game of a Memorial Day doubleheader. When the 1884 season came to a close, Williamson had clouted 27 four-baggers, and all but two came in the "friendly confines" of Lake Front Park. His home run record stood until 1919. Prior to 1884, Williamson had never hit more than three home runs in a season.

The next season found Chicago playing in West Side Park where the dimensions were not so friendly and his home run total dropped back to three. In fact, the most home runs Williamson hit after 1884 were nine, three years later.

Even though Williamson received a lot of recognition for

his power, it cannot be forgotten that he was a very good infielder, starting out as a third baseman, then moving to short. Unfortunately, his career came to an abrupt end, in of all places, Paris, France! That's right. The White Stockings were participating in baseball's first world tour, and Ed tore his kneecap while sliding into second base. The date was March 6, 1889, and even though he returned to the lineup in August of that year, Williamson was never the same player, and after the following year, was out of the game. He then developed dropsy, and his life came to a tragic end at the age of only 37.

Trivia Questions

1. Where was Williamson born?

2. Who broke his home run record?

3. What was Williamson's nickname?

4. Where did he begin his professional career at?

5. In what year?

6. How many times did Williamson lead the league in assists?

7. How many years did he lead in fielding average?

8. In what season was he switched to shortstop?

9. How many career hits did he have?

10. What was his lifetime batting average?

King Kelly

Mike "King" Kelly played with Chicago from 1880 thru 1886 and was the most popular player on the team. He was a catcher and a right fielder, and a man who never met a party that he didn't like.

Kelly won batting titles in 1884 and again in 1886 and also led the league in doubles in 1882, '83, and '84. His 155 runs scored in 1886 were a record until Rogers Hornsby scored 156 in 1929.

Despite being successful in Chicago, Kelly's off-the-field antics prompted his trade to the Boston Braves in February of 1887, for the sum of $10,000. He finished his career with the Giants in 1893.

After his playing days were over, his hard lifestyle eventually caught up with Kelly. To make a living, he started making theatrical appearances. But after giving his overcoat to a beggar in November of 1894, Kelly developed pneumonia and died a short time after turning 37.

He was elected to the Hall of Fame in 1945.

Trivia Questions

1. With what team did Kelly begin his career with?

2. How many batting championships did he win?

3. Name the years and the averages.

4. How many years did he lead the league in doubles?

5. How many years did he lead the league in runs scored?

6. Because of Kelly's base running, what popular song was heard during that day?

7. As a catcher, what innovation did he teach the Chicago pitchers?

8. What team and league did Kelly jump to in 1890?

9. How many lifetime hits did he have?

10. What was his lifetime batting average?

Bill Hutchison

After breaking in as a 29-year-old rookie for Chicago in 1889, Hutchison was a workhorse over the next few seasons. From 1890 thru 1892, he won 122 games!

In 1892, Hutchison pitched a club record 627 innings, striking out 316 batters. However, he also had some control problems, as he walked 199 in 1890.

Then in 1893, the pitching distance to home plate was increased from 50 feet to the current 60 feet, six inches. After that change, his best record was 14-15 in 1894.

Control continued to be a problem for Hutchison, and he was released by Chicago at the end of the next season. He tried an unsuccessful comeback with the Cardinals two years later, then returned to the railroad industry, where he worked until his death in 1926.

Trivia Questions

1. On what date and year was Hutchison born?

2. Where was he born?

3. What university did Hutchison graduate from?

4. What minor league team did he play for?

Chicago Cubs Facts & Trivia

5. What was his record as a rookie with Chicago in 1889?

6. How many times did he win 40 games?

7. What were the most wins he had in a season?

8. What was his nickname?

9. What feat did he accomplish on Memorial Day of 1890?

10. What was his lifetime record and his ERA?

Clark Griffith

Besides being known as the owner of the Washington Senators, Clark Griffith was a right handed pitcher with the National League Chicago White Stockings from September of 1893 thru 1900. From 1894 thru 1899, Griffith won 20 or more games. In 1898, his record was 26-10 and his ERA was a league leading 1.88.

You would think that a pitcher would be proud of a shutout. But that was not the case with Griffith, who thought throwing a shutout would bring bad luck. It wasn't until August 13, 1897, that Griffith pitched a shutout. That was his sixth season in the Majors.

Griffith was also known as a good hitter and once went 5-for-5 in a game against the Phillies. His career with the White Stockings came to an end when he jumped across town to the rival White Sox when the American League was declared a Major League in 1901. As a pitcher-manager he led the White Sox to the league's first pennant that year. Griffith also played with the New York Highlanders, who later became the Yankees, and he also played briefly with the Reds and Senators, ending his career in 1914.

Trivia Questions

1. When was Griffith born?

2. Where was he born?

3. What was the score of Griffith's first shutout?

4. Who did it come against?

5. Griffith holds the team record for the longest shutout victory. How long was it?

6. Who was the opposing pitcher?

7. What team did he play for?

8. Who drove in the winning run?

9. What was Griffith's lifetime record?

10. What was his lifetime ERA?

Jimmy Ryan

One of the greatest all-around players of his time, Jimmy Ryan broke in with the White Stockings in 1885 and played with them thru 1900. He played all three outfield positions and was one of the best outfielders of his time and in team history.

Excluding the 1887 season when walks counted as hits, Ryan batted over .300 13 times. He was also known as a power hitter. Despite standing only 5'9" and weighing 162 pounds, Ryan hit 118 home runs and led the league in four baggers in 1888. That proved to be his finest season as he led the league in five offensive categories.

But hitting and fielding weren't Ryan's only contributions. He was a very successful relief pitcher in the late 1880s and early 1890s. Following the 1900 season, Ryan was released by Chicago, but he came back to the Majors in 1902 and hit .320 at the age of 39 with the AL Washington Senators. He retired from the Major Leagues after the next season.

Trivia Questions

1. How many assists did Ryan have in the National League in his career?

2. In his first year as a regular, what was his average?

3. In 1894, Ryan had the highest average of his career. What did he hit?

4. Ryan led the league in home runs in 1888 with how many?

5. How many lead-off homers did he hit in 1889?

6. How many lifetime RBIs did he have?

7. How many times in a Chicago uniform did he score 100 or more runs?

8. What were the most runs he scored in a season?

9. In what year did he do that?

10. What was Ryan's pitching record in 1888?

11. How many of those victories came in relief?

12. How many lifetime hits did Ryan collect?

13. How many came with Chicago?

14. How many runs did he score during his career?

15. What was Ryan's lifetime batting average?

Fred Pfeffer

Fred was one of the greatest second basemen of the early days of baseball, being compared to Nap Lajoie and Eddie Collins.

Counting a year in the Players League, Pfeffer led the National League in putouts eight consecutive years from 1884 thru 1891. During that eight-year period, he also led the league in assists four times, double plays seven times, and total chances per game, seven times. He accomplished those feats without wearing a glove! It wasn't until 1896 that he started to wear the glove on a full-time basis.

Pfeffer was not a high average hitter, but he did hit in the clutch. However, he was best known as an infielder with Chicago's famed "Stonewall Infield" of the 1880s.

After his career, he coached college baseball, ran a semi-pro team, managed Decatur of the Three-I League, and also ran a baseball school. Pfeffer also operated a saloon, and when he died, he was the head press box custodian of some area race tracks.

Trivia Questions

1. Where was Pfeffer born?

2. What was his nickname?

3. He once won a gold medal for throwing a baseball how far?

4. What was his highest batting average with Chicago?

5. In what year?

6. On April 4, 1892, Pfeffer was traded to what team?

7. How many seasons did he play in the Majors?

8. What was his lifetime average?

9. How many hits did he have?

10. How many games did he play?

11. Where did he coach college baseball?

Tommy Burns

Like Pfeffer, Burns was part of the "Stonewall Infield," first as a shortstop and later as a third baseman. He was signed by Chicago in 1880 after an average minor league career and hit .309 as a rookie. Though not a spectacular player like some of his teammates, Burns was a hustler and was a favorite of his manager "Cap" Anson and the Chicago fans, who loved his head-first dives into base.

His greatest game came on September 6, 1883, when he helped set six Major League records when Chicago scored 18 runs in the bottom of the 7th inning at home against Detroit.

Burns was a shortstop until 1886, when he moved to third base. After the switch, he twice led the league in putouts, twice in assists, and once in double plays, and he was one of the premier third baseman of his time.

In 1890, Burns was one of the few Chicago players who did not jump to the Players League. During that season, he helped set another record. On August 16, in the fifth inning of a game against the Pirates, Burns and teammate Malachi Kittredge hit grand slam home runs, as Chicago romped to an 18-5 win.

After the 1891 season, he was released by Chicago and picked up by the Pirates as a player-manager. But just 55 games into the 1892 season, he was fired. Even though his playing career had ended, Tommy continued to manage, first with Springfield of the Eastern League (1893-1897), then coming back to manage Chicago in 1898. After a 4th place finish that year and with the White Stockings dropping to 8th the following year, Burns was out of a job. He then managed Buffalo of the Eastern League for a portion of the 1901 season before dying of a heart-attack while under contract to manage the Jersey City team in the Eastern League.

Trivia Questions

1. Burns broke into pro ball in 1878 with what team?

2. On September 6, 1883, Burns helped set six Major League records. How many hits did he collect in the bottom of the 7th inning?

3. How many runs did he score?

4. How many extra base hits did he have?

5. What were they?

6. How many hits did Burns have in that game?

7. What were the most RBIs he had with Chicago?

Chicago Cubs Facts & Trivia

8. What was his lifetime batting average?

9. How many hits did he have?

10. What was his record as manager of Chicago?

More Trivia Questions About That Era

1. What Chicago pitcher is credited with being a co-inventor of the curve ball?

2. How old was he?

3. Where did it occur?

4. Name the date and the year.

5. As a rookie for Chicago in 1880, this pitcher won how many games?

6. How many did he lose?

7. What kind of pitch did he throw?

8. He led the league with how many strikeouts?

9. How many starts did he have?

10. How many did he finish?

11. This same pitcher also became the first in the franchise to throw a no-hitter. Who did it come against?

12. John Clarkson won 327 Major League games. How many came with Chicago?

13. How many did he lose with Chicago?

14. On July 27, 1885, Clarkson pitched a no-hitter against what team?

15. On September 19 of that same year, he did what?

16. How many games did Clarkson win that season?

17. How many did he lose?

18. How many innings did he pitch?

19. How many strikeouts did he have?

20. Out of 70 starts, how many games did he complete?

21. How many shutouts did he have?

22. How many games did Clarkson win in 1886?

23. How many strikeouts did he have that season?

24. How many games did he win in 1887?

25. Clarkson was sold to what team in 1888?

26. How much money was he sold for?

27. What year was Clarkson elected to the Baseball Hall of Fame?

28. What right-handed Chicago pitcher won 14-straight games in 1885?

29. This same pitcher won how many consecutive games the

following year?

30. This left-handed Chicago pitcher walked 16 batters in 1887. Who was he?

31. Against what team did he walk the 16 batters in a single game?

32. He also pitched a no-hitter into the bottom of the 7th inning against what team?

33. On what date did that occur?

34. This same pitcher also played the outfield and hit for what average in 1889?

35. Hugh Duffy played one year with the Cubs. What was the year?

36. What was his average that year?

37. How many home runs did he hit that season?

38. This former Chicago White Stocking had back to back hitting streaks of 42 and 28 games. Who was he?

39. What year did he accomplish this feat?

40. What was his nickname?

41. How many years did Billy Sunday play with the White Stockings?

42. What was his highest batting average?

43. Against what team did he make his Major League debut?

44. What pitcher struck him out four times in four at bats that day?

45. After Chicago, what team did Sunday play for?

46. He wound up his career with what team?

47. After Sunday's career came to an end, he became an evangelist. How long did he do that?

48. How many times was he married?

49. In 1890, Walt Wilmot led the National League in home runs with how many?

50. What position did he play?

51. On August 22, 1891, Wilmot accomplished what?

52. He did that against what team?

53. In 1894, Wilmot had his best big league season. What was his average?

54. How many runs did he score that season?

55. How many RBIs did he have that year?

56. He set a club record in hits in 1894. How many did Wilmot have?

57. After leaving Chicago, he played two seasons with what team?

58. What was Wilmot's lifetime average?

Chicago Cubs Facts & Trivia

59. How many years did George Decker play with Chicago?

60. His best year was 1894. What was his average?

61. How many RBIs did he have that season?

62. On July 25 of that year, he did what against the Pirates?

63. How long did Bill Lange play with Chicago?

64. How many bases did he steal in 1896?

65. In 1897, he led the league in stolen bases with how many?

66. What was Lange's batting average in 1895?

67. How many runs did he score that season?

68. How many home runs did he hit that year?

69. Lange retired after the 1899 season. What was his lifetime average?

70. How many hits did he have?

71. How many lifetime stolen bases did he have?

72. How old was Lange when he retired?

73. Lange was born and he died in the same city. What was the city?

74. This player became the first Major League player to catch a baseball that was dropped from the Washington Monument. Who was he?

75. How many tries did it take?

76. What was his career batting average?

77. Bill Everett holds the team record for highest batting average by a rookie. What did he hit?

78. What year was it?

79. He also shared a team record for most hits in a season in the 19th Century. How many did he have?

80. Who does he share that record with?

81. As a third baseman, how many errors did Everett make in 1895?

82. He was switched to what position in 1898?

83. How many career hits did he have?

84. What was his lifetime batting average?

85. On June 29, 1887, Chicago set a record for runs scored in a single game. How many did they score?

86. Who did they beat?

87. What was William McCormick's nickname?

88. On May 18, 1898, this pitcher hit three consecutive batters. Name him.

89. What team was he pitching against?

90. What was the nickname of Edward Green?

91. What was his lifetime average?

92. How many hits did he have?

93. Besides playing the outfield, what other position did Sam Mertes play?

94. In what year did he start playing for Chicago?

95. On June 8 and 9, 1900, he accomplished what feat?

96. He played with the White Sox and the Giants and then finished his career with what team?

97. How many years did Mertes play in the Majors?

98. What was his lifetime batting average?

99. This player was the only one to play under both Cap Anson and Frank Chance. Who was he?

100. What was his nickname?

4
THE EARLY YEARS OF THE 20TH CENTURY

The National League had been in existence since 1876, but a new league emerged at the dawn of the 20th Century.

The American League was formed in 1900. The AL's president, Ban Johnson, declared it to be a Major League the following year, and the war was begun for the established stars of the National League. Chicago was one of the hardest hit, and as a result, finished 6th in 1901.

Former Boston manager Frank Selee was named the team's new manager in 1902, and he instituted a change in the makeup of the team. He emphasized a "youth movement", which eventually resulted in a nickname change for the team. The NL Chicago White Stockings became the Chicago Cubs in a few years, and that moniker has stuck ever since.

In 1902, another tradition began. Shortstop Joe Tinker joined the club as did second baseman Johnny Evers. When catcher Frank Chance was moved from catcher to first base, the famous phrase, "Tinkers to Evers to Chance," was born. Their first double play was recorded on September 15 of that year. The 1902 Cubs finished 5th and by the following year had crept up to 3rd. The rise continued to 2nd place in 1904. That finish was aided by the acquisition of Mordecai Brown and outfielder Frank Schulte. In 1905, Chicago slipped to 3rd, behind pennant-winning New York and 2nd place Pittsburgh.

The Cubs also lost their manager Frank Selee that year, as he resigned on August 1 because of poor health. The players elected Frank Chance as the new manager.

During the off-season, the Cubs acquired third baseman Harry Steinfeldt, left fielder Jimmy Sheckard, and left handed pitcher Jack Pfiester. Those acquisitions plus a few other players propelled Chicago to the top of the league. The Cubs won pennants in 1906, 1907, 1908, and 1910 and the World Series in 1907 and 1908. The 1906 team won a record 116 games but lost the series in six games to the White Sox.

After dominating the league for five years, the Cubs started to age and slipped to 2nd place in 1911 and 3rd the following season. In September 1912, Chance was fired as manager. Despite the addition of some new stars, the Cubs finished 3rd again in 1913 and 4th the next two seasons. The team also changed ownership as Charles Murphy was bought out by Charles Thomas following the 1913 campaign.

At the close of 1915, attendance had dwindled on the west side and the future did not look promising.

SOME STARS OF THAT ERA

Frank Chance

Frank Chance began his big league career with Chicago on April 29, 1898. His first game certainly wasn't impressive. Inserted into the lineup as a catcher in the late innings against Louisville, Chance dropped two pop-ups. However, Chicago had the game in hand and won easily, 16-2. His debut as a hitter on May 11 was equally unimpressive, as he went hitless in two trips to the plate against the immortal Cy Young of Cleveland.

Until the latter part of the 1902 season, Chance saw very little action as the team's backup catcher, but then new manager Frank Selee started playing Chance at first base, a position he didn't like at first! But that feeling was short-lived, and he went on to become a very fine first baseman.

Chance was appointed team captain in 1904, and the following year was elected, in a close vote by his teammates, to succeed the ailing Selee. He was a fierce competitor with a burning desire to win. In his first full season at the helm in 1906, the Cubs had one of the greatest seasons of all time, winning a record 116 games. The only downfall that year was their failure to win the World Series. The Cubs cross-town rival, the White Sox, dubbed the "Hitless Wonders," surprised the baseball world by knocking off the Cubs. It was a bitter defeat for Chance and his team, but they failed to let it affect their play and dominated the National League over the next few seasons.

As manager, Chance was known for being a strict disciplinarian and often settled disputes with his fists. On July 8, 1907, angered at Brooklyn fans for throwing pop bottles at his players, Chance started flinging them back into the stands. One fan suffered a lacerated leg, and after the Cubs won the game, 5-0, Chance left the stadium in an armored car that was surrounded by police.

In 1909, he suffered a broken shoulder, and his playing career began to wane. A few years later Vic Saier took over for Chance at first base. Finally, Chance was released as manager on September 28, 1912.

After leaving Chicago, Chance spent the next two seasons as player-manager of the Yankees. Almost a decade later in 1923, he surfaced again to manage the Boston Red Sox, but for only a season. During the off season, he was hired to manage the White Sox, but was unable to because of poor health.

During his career, Chance often let himself be hit by a pitch to help his teammates. In the end, it may have caught up with him, for he suffered from migraine headaches and died at the age of 47.

Trivia Questions

1. How many stolen bases did Chance have in 1903?

2. On June 13, 1904, Chance did what?

3. Chance was known for his willingness to get be hit by a pitch. During a doubleheader on May 30, 1904, how many times was he hit by a pitch?

4. What was his batting average in 1903?

5. What was Chance's average during the 1908 World Series?

6. From 1906 thru 1910, how many games did the Cubs win?

7. What was the teams winning percentage?

8. What was Chance's lifetime batting average?

9. How many hits did he have?

10. How many stolen bases did he have?

11. When was Chance elected to the Baseball Hall of Fame?

12. What teammates were also elected at the same time?

Johnny Kling

Kling was born on February 25, 1875 in Kansas City, Missouri, and died there on January 31, 1947. Although only 5' 9½" and 160 pounds, Kling developed into a force behind the plate. However, that wasn't his position when he broke into professional baseball with Houston of the Texas League. At that time, he was an outfielder.

In 1900 he was playing with St. Joseph of the Western League, where he hit .301. Later that year, he signed on with the Cubs.

In 1902, Kling sewed up the catcher's spot with superb fielding to go along with a .286 batting average. From that point on, he was the best receiver in the National League and led the league in a number of defensive categories. His baseball future shone bright until he gave it up temporarily for another game. Kling retired from baseball after winning the world pocket billiard title during the winter of 1908-09 and decided to leave the game. But it was only a temporary respite. After losing the billiard championship the next time around, Kling decided to come back to the Cubs in 1910. His return sparked the club to another pennant, even though Chicago lost the World Series.

However, not everyone was happy about Kling's return. Owner Charles Murphy was not happy about his leaving baseball for billiards and traded him to Boston in June of 1911. Kling played through two seasons with Boston, serving as player-manager in 1912, before being traded to the Reds to finish out his career in 1913.

After his career was over, Kling operated a few pool halls in the Kansas City area and died there in 1947.

Trivia Questions

1. Kling excelled from 1902 thru 1908. During that time, how many years did he lead the league in fielding average?

2. How many times in putouts?

3. How many years in assists?

4. How many times in double plays?

5. Who replaced King as catcher in 1909?

6. When did Kling make his Major League debut?

7. Against what team?

8. How many hits did he have in his first Major League game?

9. What was his lifetime average?

10. How many career hits did he have?

11. How many stolen bases?

Johnny Evers

Evers was one of the best second baseman of all time. The Cubs got him cheap, paying only $250 for his contract in 1902. Finishing out that season, Evers hit just .222, not even doubling his weight of 125 pounds!

But Evers made up for his lack of size with a lot of determination and hustle. Early in 1903, Bobby Lowe, the regular second baseman, broke his leg, and Evers took over. From that point on, the job was his. He continued his standout play for the Cubs and took over as manager in 1913. Evers's Cubs finished 3rd that year, but he was fired by owner Charles Murphy. However, Evers was not to be denied a comeback. He was picked up by the Boston Braves in 1914 and became part of their "Miracle Braves" team that won the pennant and took the World Series. Evers hit .438 during the Series as Boston swept Philadelphia in four straight games! He drove home a Chalmers automobile for his efforts.

Chicago Cubs Facts & Trivia

By 1917, Evers had been released to the Phillies. He returned to manage the Cubs in 1921 for most of the season and for the White Sox in 1924. Following those unsuccessful seasons, Evers served in civilian capacities with a number of teams. He died after suffering a second stroke in 1947.

Trivia Questions

1. When was Evers born?

2. Where was he born?

3. What were his nicknames?

4. How many stolen bases did he have in 1906?

5. How many did he have in 1907?

6. In 1908, he led the Cubs in hitting. What was his average?

7. What was Evers lifetime batting average?

8. How many hits did he have?

9. How many stolen bases did have?

10. Where is Evers buried at?

Joe Tinker

Tinker played 11 years as shortstop for the Cubs, and after a 1902 rookie season, in which he led the National League in errors, he became one of the top defensive players in the league. The only other shortstop who was better was the

Pirates' Honus Wagner. Enough said!

Tinker wasn't a high average hitter but he came through in the clutch. He was also a swift and clever base runner, stealing 304 bases with the Cubs.

One of his greatest offensive games came against one of the greatest pitchers of all time, Christy Mathewson. On August 7, 1911, Tinker went 4-for-4, including two singles, a double, and a triple. He also stole home and turned two double plays in an 8-6 Cub victory.

Tinker, like many players of his era, could be a fighter if he had to. He and teammate Johnny Evers had an on-the-field brawl in 1905, which left them not speaking to each other for several years. However, it didn't affect their play on the field.

Tinker was granted a trade to Cincinnati after Evers was made Cub manager in the winter of 1912-13. He served as player-manger of the Reds and compiled his best single season average of .317, even though Cincinnati finished 7th.

In 1915, Tinker jumped to the Federal League, and as a player-manager, he led the Chicago Whales to a pennant. After the Federal League folded, Tinker came back to the Cubs as a player-manager in 1916 but was fired after the club finished 5th.

After leaving the Major Leagues, Tinker played briefly with Columbus of the American Association; then in 1921, settled in Orlando, Florida.

Tinker, along with Evers and Chance, were elected to the Baseball Hall of Fame in 1946.

Trivia Questions

1. When was Tinker born?

2. Where was he born?

3. How tall was he and what was his weight?

Chicago Cubs Facts & Trivia

4. On October 11, 1908, Tinker became the first Cub to do what?

5. How many stolen bases did he have in 1904?

6. On June 28, 1910, Tinker accomplished what?

7. How many times did he lead the league in fielding average?

8. How many times did he lead in total chances?

9. How many times did he lead the league in putouts?

10. How many times in double plays?

11. What was his lifetime batting average?

Mordecai Brown

This Hall of Fame pitcher was born in Nyesville, Indiana, and grew up to be one of the greatest right handed pitchers of all time. He achieved his nickname, "Three Finger" Brown, because of a childhood farming accident. The loss of part of his index finger allowed him to put more spin on the ball. Batters had a hard time hitting his curve ball which broke down and out.

Brown broke into the Majors with the Cardinals in 1903 and was just 9-13. But his record that year didn't deter Cubs manager Frank Selee, who liked the way Brown's pitches moved, from trading away 20-game-winner Jack Taylor for him. The trade proved to be very beneficial for the Cubs during their heyday from 1906-1910. Brown was their top pitcher, and starting in 1906, he won 20 games or more for six consecutive seasons. Another highlight of Brown's career was his mastery over the Giants and their pitching ace, Christy Mathewson. Their most important duel occurred on October 8, 1908. It was a one game playoff at the Polo Grounds to determine the National League pennant. Brown was called in to relieve starter Jack Pfiester with two on and two out in the bottom half of the 1st inning and with one Giant run having already crossed the plate. Brown struck out the next batter and finished the game as the Cubs won, 4-2. Several Cub players were roughed up by an angry New York mob after the game, forcing police protection.

In the World Series, Brown won two games as the Cubs took Detroit in five games.

After a 5-6 record in 1912, Brown was sold to Cincinnati for the 1913 season, and the following year, he jumped to the new Federal League. When that league folded, Brown came back to the Cubs in 1916. It seemed only fitting that "Three Finger" pitched his last major league game against his old rival, Christy Mathewson. However, the game resembled nothing of their earlier classic matchups, and the nearly 40-year-old Brown was beaten by Mathewson, 10-8.

Brown later bounced around the minor leagues where he pitched and managed until 1920.

Trivia Questions

1. What position did Brown play before he became a pitcher?

2. What were the most wins he had in a season?

3. What year was that?

4. How many consecutive games did Brown win in 1906?

5. How many shutouts did he have that season?

6. How many career shutouts did he have?

7. How many games did Brown pitch against Christy Mathewson?

8. How many did "Three Finger" win?

9. How many games in a row did he win against Mathewson?

10. What was Brown's lifetime record?

11. How many one-hitters did he have?

12. Where did Brown die?

13. In what year was he elected to the Hall of Fame?

14. How many world series games did Brown win?

Frank Schulte

Frank Schulte was one of the Cubs' best all around players in the early 1900s. He came to Chicago in September 1904 and in 20 games hit .286. The following year Schulte became the regular left fielder and hit .274. A year later he was moved to right field and upped his average to .281 and led the league with 13 triples.

Schulte was also involved in a strange play that turned the tide of that fall's World Series. The White Sox were leading the series, three games to two. In the bottom of the 1st inning, the Cubs were ahead, 1-0, when George Davis came to the plate with one out and runners on first and second. Davis hit a drive to deep right field that Schulte was unable to come up with. The Cubs right fielder always claimed that, while he was waiting to catch the ball, a policeman pushed him. Manager Frank Chance wanted Davis to be called out because of fan interference, but the hit was ruled a double. The White Sox went on to win the game, 8-3, and in the process, won the World Series.

Schulte had his greatest year in 1911, leading the league in home runs, RBIs and slugging percentage. But after that season, his production fell off, and finally in 1916, he was traded to the Pirates. After playing briefly with the Phillies, Schulte finished his career with the Senators in 1918.

Trivia Questions

1. What was Schulte's nickname?

2. What was his batting average in the 1908 World Series?

3. What famous Chicago *Tribune* sportswriter became good friends with Schulte?

4. In 1910, he hit the most home runs in a season by a Cub in 15 years. How many did he hit?

5. Schulte led the league with how many home runs in 1911?

6. How many RBIs did he have that season?

7. How many runs did he score in 1911?

8. How many doubles did he hit that year?

9. How many triples did he have in 1911?

10. What was his average and slugging percentage that season?

Chicago Cubs Facts & Trivia 49

11. How many stolen bases did he have that year?

12. During the 1911 season, Schulte became the first player to do what?

13. He also set a record for most grand slams in a season. How many did he hit?

14. How long did that record last?

15. How many career hits did he have?

16. What was his lifetime batting average?

Heinie Zimmerman

Heinie played with the Cubs from 1907 thru 1916 as a third baseman. However, he also made a number of appearances at second base and occasionally played shortstop or first base.

Besides being good in the field, Heinie was an excellent hitter. His greatest year came in 1912 when he led the league in hitting and home runs. There are also some sources that list him as the RBI leader. However, Honus Wagner is recognized as the RBI leader that season, so Heinie did not officially win the triple crown.

Zimmerman had many highlights through the years for the Cubs before being traded to the Giants in August, 1916. He promptly helped New York win the pennant the following year, but then became the goat of the World Series, when he chased the White Sox's Eddie Collins across the plate with what proved to be the winning run in the 6th and final game of the series. However, on the play, New York had no one at home plate to throw the ball to, so Heinie should not have taken all the blame.

Zimmerman played two more years with the Giants before his career came to an end for being implicated in some betting scandals.

Trivia Questions

1. Zimmerman led the National League in hitting in 1912. What was his average?

2. That season he also became the first Cub to collect 200 hits in a season. How many did he have?

3. How many home runs did he hit that year?

4. How many RBIs was Zimmerman officially credited with in 1912?

5. He also had a nice hitting streak that season. How long was it?

6. What team record did Heinie set on June 11, 1911?

7. What team were the Cubs playing?

8. What happened to Zimmerman three times, in a five game period in 1913?

9. How many lifetime hits did he have?

10. What was his career batting average?

Chicago Cubs Facts & Trivia

More Trivia Questions About That Era

1. From June 20, 1901 thru August 9, 1906, this Cub pitcher displayed his durability. Who was he and what did he do?

2. What was his nickname?

3. What percentage of his lifetime starts did he complete?

4. This manager guided the Cubs in 1900 and 1901. Who was he?

5. How did his teams finish?

6. In 1901, this Cub left fielder played his only season with the Cubs. Who was he?

7. What was his nickname?

8. He led Chicago in batting that year. What was his average?

9. How many hits did he have that season?

10. What team did he play for in 1902?

11. Rube Waddell pitched with the Cubs in 1901. What was his record?

12. What was Carl Lundgren's lifetime record?

13. In what years did he pitch for the Cubs?

14. What was his ERA in 1907?

15. On September 15, 1902, Lundgren was on the mound against the Reds. Besides the Cubs winning, 6-3, something else occurred that day. What was it?

16. What was Lundgren's nickname?

17. Why did he get it?

18. After leaving the Cubs and bouncing around the minors for a few seasons, Lundgren later did what?

19. After Frank Selee took over as manager in 1902, the team became known as the Cubs. But Selee preferred another name. What was it?

20. Jimmy Slagle had two nicknames. What were they?

21. He led the league in assists in 1905. How many did he have?

22. Slagle stole how many bases in the 1907 World Series?

23. How many years did he play in the Majors?

24. What was Slagle's lifetime batting average?

25. How many stolen bases did he have?

26. How many career home runs did he hit in his career?

27. What was Jake Weimer's lifetime pitching record?

28. What other teams did he play for besides the Cubs?

29. What was his nickname?

Chicago Cubs Facts & Trivia

30. What was Bob Wicker's lifetime record?

31. Wicker pitched a nine inning no-hitter against the Giants on June 11, 1904. Wicker finally won, 1-0, in 12 innings. Who did he beat?

32. What team did Wicker break in with?

33. What was his record in 1903?

34. What pitcher did the Cubs trade him for?

35. Artie Hofman played every position for the Cubs except what two?

36. What year did he begin playing for the Cubs?

37. What was Hofman's nickname?

38. What was his average in the 1906 World Series?

39. In 1909, he became a starter at what position?

40. What was his average that season?

41. Hofman's best year was 1910. What was his average?

42. How many hits did he have in his career?

43. What was his lifetime average?

44. Pitcher Ed Reulbach joined the Cubs in 1905. What was his record his rookie year?

45. What was his nickname?

46. On August 24, 1905, Ed beat the Phillies, 2-1. How many innings did he pitch in that game?

47. What was his record in 1906?

48. In that season, Reulbach won how many games in a row?

49. On October 10, 1906, in the World Series against the White Sox, what did Ed accomplish?

50. This feat remained unduplicated until what year?

51. What was Reulbach's record in 1908?

52. On September 26 of that year, he did what?

53. How many times has that been accomplished?

54. Who did he beat?

55. What were the scores?

56. How many consecutive shutouts did he have in 1908?

57. How long did that record stand?

58. In 1909, Reulbach won how many games in a row?

59. What was his lifetime record?

60. Orval Overall made his Major League debut with what team?

61. In what year was he traded to the Cubs?

Chicago Cubs Facts & Trivia

62. He was the first graduate of what university to make it to the big leagues?

63. What was his record with the Cubs his first year?

64. Overall's best season came in 1907. What was his record?

65. What was his ERA that season?

66. How many shutouts did he have?

67. In winning his first World Series game against the Tigers, Overall pitched a five-hitter. What was the score?

68. How many games did he win during the regular season in 1909?

69. That season he led the league with how many strikeouts?

70. Overall became the last Cub pitcher to strike out over 200 batters until who accomplished the feat and in what year?

71. What was Overall's lifetime record?

72. What was his lifetime ERA?

73. How many years did he play in the Majors?

74. Jimmy Sheckard led the National League in walks in 1911 with how many walks?

75. His walk total that season remained a league record until what year?

76. Who broke it?

77. What years did Sheckard play with the Cubs?

78. What position did he play with Chicago?

79. This Cub led the team in hitting in 1906. Who was he?

80. What was his average?

81. Where was Jimmy Archer born?

82. What position did he play?

83. What technique did he develop, which ironically kept him from reaching the Major Leagues for several seasons?

84. How many years did he play with the Cubs?

85. In 1912, how many men did Archer throw out trying to steal?

86. What was "King" Cole's first name?

87. How many games did he win in his rookie year?

88. On July 31, 1910, what did Cole do?

89. What other factor was unique about that game?

90. What was his lifetime record?

91. In 1912, this rookie Cubs pitcher was 26-10. Who was he?

92. How many complete games did he have that season?

Chicago Cubs Facts & Trivia

93. On September 14, 1913, this same Cubs pitcher shutout the Giants on how many hits?

94. Who had the first pinch-hit home run in Cub history?

95. What pitcher did it come against?

96. This Cubs pitcher threw a 2-0 no-hitter against the Giants at the Polo Grounds on August 31, 1915. Who was he?

97. What pitch was he noted for?

98. Roger Bresnahan played what position before becoming a catcher?

99. He was the first catcher to use what kind of protective gear?

100. What National League team did he break in with?

101. When did he come to Chicago?

102. When did Bresnahan rejoin the Cubs?

103. In 1915, he became player-manager of Chicago. What place did the Cubs finish in?

104. In what year was Bresnahan inducted into the Hall of Fame?

105. Who managed the Cubs in 1914?

106. Besides being a player and managing in the Major Leagues, what else was O'Day famous for?

5
WRIGLEY TAKES OVER

Charles Weeghman, who had been the owner of the Federal League Chicago Whales, became the controlling owner of the Cubs in 1916 after buying a majority interest in the club as part of the settlement between the upstart league and the established circuits.

Chewing gum magnate William Wrigley, Jr., also bought a piece of the action by investing $50,000. Two years later Wrigley became majority owner, then in 1921, he took over sole ownership of the team.

The Cubs moved to what is now Wrigley Field in 1916. The park had been built in 1914 for the Chicago Whales of the short-lived Federal League, and when the Cubs moved in, it was called Weeghman Park. It was renamed Wrigley Field in 1926.

The Cubs finished 5th in both 1916 and 1917, but in the off season, they picked up some much needed help. Pitchers Grover Alexander from the Phillies and Lefty Tyler from the Braves were acquired as was Alexander's catcher, Bill Killefer. Outfielder George Paskert was also picked up from the Phillies, and shortstop Charlie Hollocher was brought up from the minor leagues. In 1918, the Cubs jumped all the way to 1st place without the help of Alexander, who was drafted into the Army after pitching just three games. But the Cubs were beaten in the World Series by the Red Sox in six games, even though Chicago outscored Boston, 10-9.

In 1919, Chicago dropped to 3rd place and followed that

up with 5th and 7th place finishes. Johnny Evers replaced Fred Mitchell as manager for the 1921 season, but Evers was replaced in August of that year by Bill Killefer. The Cubs stayed consistant for a few seasons, finishing 5th in 1922, 4th in 1923, and 5th in 1924. There were a few old faces left on the team, but a number of new players were added, including first baseman Ray Grimes, infielder Sparky Adams, third baseman Barney Friberg, and outfielders Hack Miller and Jigger Statz. But in 1925, the Cubs slid to last for the first time in their 50 years in the National League, despite having three different managers. More changes would be coming as Chicago struggled to turn things around.

SOME PLAYERS OF THE TEENS AND '20S

Grover Alexander

Grover "Pete" Alexander joined the Cubs after his most productive years were behind him, but he still won 128 for Chicago. In his first season in 1918, Alexander won two of three games before being drafted by the Army.

After serving in France, he came back to the Cubs in 1919. However, a number of things had occurred to Alexander in the time he was gone to war. For one, he had been gassed on the battlefield and had also suffered a partial hearing loss. Then, shortly after returning home, he started drinking heavily and also developed epilepsy. "Pete" would suffer seizures in the dugout but for some strange reason, never had any while he was on the mound.

But despite all of his problems, Alexander had some great seasons for the Cubs. In 1919, he threw nine shutouts en route to a 16-11 record. The following year, he led the league in wins with 27 and in the process had a nine-game winning streak.

He continued his winning ways for Chicago until he was

Chicago Cubs Facts & Trivia

sent to the Cardinals on waivers in June of 1926. He played with St. Louis through the 1929 season before returning to the Phillies the following season to finish his big league career.

After his playing days were over, "Pete" continued to suffer seizures and spent a lot of time in sanitariums. He was elected to the Hall of Fame in 1937 and was at the dediciation of the Cooperstown shrine in 1939.

Alexander died in 1950.

Trivia Questions

1. From April 18 thru May 13, 1923, how many consecutive innings did Alexander pitch without issuing a walk?

2. On September 21, 1919, he pitched the shortest game in Cubs history. How long was it?

3. Who did he beat?

4. What was the score?

5. How many innings did he pitch in 1920?

6. What was his ERA that year?

7. How many strikeouts did he have?

8. On what date did Alexander win his 300th game?

9. Who did it come against?

10. What was the score?

11. In the 1925 City Series between the Cubs and the White Sox, Alexander and the White Sox's Ted Blankenship,

pitched a 2-2 tie. How long did the game last?

12. What was Grover's middle name?

Bill Killefer

Although a long time player and also a manager, Killefer's greatest claim to fame is that he was the batterymate of Grover Alexander. He also accompanied Alexander on the trade that sent them both from the Phillies to the Cubs. However, his career strictly as a player was almost over.

On August 21, 1921, Killefer took over as Cub manager, replacing Johnny Evers. The Cubs finished that season in 7th place but climbed to fifth the following season with a record of 80-74. Chicago finished 4th in 1923, then sank to 5th the following season. However, during both years, the Cubs record was above .500. But by mid-1925 with the Cubs at the bottom of the league, Killefer was fired.

He later coached and managed in the big leagues and also managed in the minors before retiring.

Trivia Questions

1. Where was Killefer born?

2. When was he born?

3. What was his nickname?

4. Who was the first Major League team he played with?

5. What was the year?

6. When did he join the Phillies?

7. How much money did the Cubs pay for Grover Alexander and Killefer?

8. What was Killefer's batting average in the 1918 World Series?

9. What was his managerial record with the Cubs?

10. How old was Killefer when he died?

Hack Miller

Miller was born in New York City, but from the age of one, he was raised in Chicago. Hack was known for his strength that was inherited from his father who had been a circus strong-man.

He began his baseball career with some semi-pro teams in Chicago before breaking in with Wausau of the Wisconsin-Illinois League in 1914. He later played for several teams in the Northern League before the Dodgers brought him to the Majors two years later. After another two years, Miller was brought up to the Big Leagues again, this time by the Boston Red Sox. However, he still wasn't ready for the big time, so he went back to the minors.

After hitting .346 in 1919 and .347 the following two seasons, Miller signed with the Cubs for the 1922 season. As a left fielder that year, he hit .352 with 12 home runs and 78 RBIs and helped lead the Cubs to 5th place. The next year Miller slugged 20 homers, drove in 88 runs and hit .301. On June 12 of that year, he hit two home runs and a single and drove in seven runs to lead the Cubs to a 12-11 win over the Braves at Wrigley Field. In 1924, Miller hit .336 but appeared in just 53 games, mainly because he was just an average fielder who wasn't able to cover a lot of ground in the outfield. On May 21, 1925, he batted for the final time as a Cub and slugged a run-scoring pinch-hit triple in a 5-4 loss to Brooklyn. He was released three days later, then went to the minor leagues before retiring in 1927. In just 349 Major League games, Miller had 387 hits and batted .323.

Trivia Questions

1. What was Hack's real first name?

2. How did he get his nickname?

3. How many hits did Miller have in 1922?

4. How heavy were his bats?

5. What was his lifetime average as a pinch hitter?

6. Hack also entertained as a strong man. Once, he pounded a spike through a gate at Wrigley field. His fist was protected by what?

7. How big was he?

8. What did he hit in his last big league season with the Cubs?

9. Where did he die?

10. When did he die?

Hippo Vaughn

Vaughn ranks 5th on the Cubs all-time list with 151 wins and the most by a Chicago left-hander.

The Cubs acquired Vaughn in August 1913 for another

pitcher, Lew Richie. Before coming to Chicago, he had played briefly with the Yankees and the Senators over a five-year period. But once coming to the Cubs, Vaughn's career took off.

In 1914, he was 21-13. With the exception of 1916, when he won 17 games, Vaughn was a 20-game winner thru 1919. He had a good fastball and registered 195 strikeouts in 1917, the year he won 23 games, the highest one season total of his career. However, 1918 was his best all around year, as Vaughn led the league in wins, ERA, innings pitched, strikeouts, shutouts, and games started. Even though he lost two out of three games to the Boston Red Sox in the World Series, his ERA was just 1.00 in 27 innings of work.

Vaughn's career with the Cubs ended during the 1921 season when he quit the team. At the time, his record had slipped to 3-11, but he also did not get along with new manager Johnny Evers. Their mutual dislike for each other went all the way back to 1913 when Evers had previously managed Chicago.

After his Major League career was over, Vaughn pitched for a number of semi-pro teams in Chicago and later returned to the Cubs as a batting practice pitcher in 1937.

Trivia Questions

1. What was "Hippo's" real first name?

2. On May 2, 1917, "Hippo" and Fred Toney of the Reds did what?

3. Who won the game and in what inning?

4. What was the score?

5. How many wins did Vaughn have in 1918?

6. How many strikeouts?

7. How many shutouts that season?

8. What was his ERA that year?

9. How many innings did he pitch?

10. How many games did he start in 1918?

11. How many one hit shutouts did he throw in his career?

12. On August 9, 1919, what did Vaughn do?

13. What was the score of his lone win against the Red Sox in the 1918 World Series?

14. What was his lifetime record?

15. What was his lifetime earned run average?

Fred Mitchell

Although Mitchell never played with the Cubs, he did become their manager and was a successful one at that.

His playing career was spent with a number of teams. Mitchell was a member of Boston's first American League team in 1901 and, as a pitcher, went 6-6. As a spare infielder, he hit just .159. The next year he was traded to the Philadelphia Athletics, where he went 5-8 and hit only .184. In 1903, Mitchell went to the Phillies and was used only as a pitcher. His record that year was 10-15. In 1904, he once again found himself in a different uniform, becoming a Dodger. In 1905, an arm injury forced an end to his Major League pitching career.

After bouncing around the minor leagues, Mitchell made it back to the big time in 1910 as a catcher. But his hitting was still a problem. He only hit .230 for the New York Highlanders which was not enough to keep him in the Majors. His final fling came in 1913 when he was a player-coach with the Boston Braves. He had one hit in three at bats as a pinch-hitter, but the next year helped in a greater capacity by coaching the Braves pitchers and catchers during their "miracle" season.

He became the Cubs manager in 1917, replacing Joe Tinker. In 1918, Chicago won the NL pennant but lost the World Series to Babe Ruth and the Boston Red Sox. Mitchell, as a manager, was a strategist and actually developed the "Williams Shift." It was used for former Cub Cy Williams, who was traded to the Phillies in 1918. When Williams, a left-handed pull-hitter, came to the plate, Mitchell moved the shortstop and center fielder to the right of second base. The same shift was used by Cleveland Indians manager Lou Boudreau years later against the Red Sox's Ted Williams. Boudreau has been credited with creating the "Williams Shift", but in fact, Mitchell did it years before.

For a short time, Mitchell was both manager and president of the Cubs, but the National League stepped in and said he couldn't do both. William Veeck, Sr., who had been vice-president, then took over as team president. When Mitchell left the Cubs, he managed the Boston Braves for three years, then left the Majors to coach the Harvard baseball team, a job he held until retiring in 1939.

Trivia Questions

1. What was Mitchell's real last name?

2. How did he come up with the name Mitchell?

3. Why did he change his name?

4. How many years did he manage the Cubs?

5. How many pennants did he win?

6. Name the team's season finishes in order with Mitchell at the helm?

7. What was his won-loss record as Cub manager?

8. What was his record as Harvard's head coach?

9. What was his Major League pitching record?

10. How old was Mitchell when he died?

More Questions About This Era

1. Who did Vic Saier replace at first base?

2. In what year did Saier join the Cubs?

3. His greatest season came in 1913. How many home runs did he have?

4. Saier also led the league in triples that year with how many?

5. How many homers did Saier hit in 1914?

6. Four of his home runs in 1914 came off what great pitcher?

7. How many lifetime home runs did he hit off this pitcher?

8. What was his lifetime average?

9. Why did his career with the Cubs end?

Chicago Cubs Facts & Trivia

10. In what year did Saier retire?

11. What was the last team he played on?

12. Cy Williams joined the Cubs in 1912 at the age of 24. How many years did he play in the minors?

13. After becoming a starter in 1915, he led the Cubs in home runs with how many?

14. In 1916, Williams shared the home run title with Dave Robertson of the Giants. How many did he hit?

15. Williams was traded after the 1917 season to the Phillies for what player?

16. He hit 251 home runs in his career. How many came as a Cub?

17. He managed in the minor leagues for one season in 1931 and then retired from baseball to do what?

18. What position did Williams play?

19. What position did Bob O'Farrell play?

20. How old was he when he played his first Major League game with Chicago?

21. What was his average in 1922?

22. How many runs did he drive in during the 1923 season?

23. After suffering a fractured skull from a foul tip in 1924, he only ended up playing in 71 games. Who replaced him at catcher?

24. What team was O'Farrell traded to?

25. Who did he throw out attempting to steal second base, to end the 1926 World Series?

26. What was pitcher Phil Douglas's nickname?

27. On Memorial Day in 1922, this Cub was traded to the Cardinals in between games of a doubleheader. Who was he?

28. Who did the Cubs get in return?

29. What was pitcher Claude Hendrix's record in 1918?

30. How did his career end?

31. In what year did the Cubs acquire Fred Merkle?

32. How many years did start at first base for Chicago?

33. Turner Barber played with the Cubs from 1917 thru 1922. What was his batting average in 1921?

34. This Cub pitcher went 5-for-5 on May 6, 1922. Who was he?

35. What were the hits?

36. What position did Charlie Hollocher play?

37. He led the team in hitting as a rookie in 1918. What was his average?

38. Hollocher led the league in hits with how many?

Chicago Cubs Facts & Trivia

39. His best season came in 1922. What was his average?

40. How many hits did he have?

41. How many times did Hollocher strike out that season?

42. He retired because of mysterious stomach ailments at what age?

43. What was his lifetime batting average?

44. How did he die?

45. Outfielder George Paskert became a hero in the winter of 1919-20 for doing what?

46. What was George Tyler's pitching record in 1918?

47. How many shutouts did he have that season?

48. What did Tyler do on July 17, 1918?

49. Barney Friberg broke into the Majors with the Cubs in what year?

50. What was his batting average in 1923?

51. During his career, the versatile Friberg played how many different positions?

52. This Cubs pitcher was the starter and the winner in the highest scoring game in Major League history. Who was he?

53. Who did the Cubs play?

54. What was the score?

55. This player was the Cubs starting second baseman from 1920 thru 1922. Who was he?

56. Dave Robertson played as a regular for one season with the Cubs in 1920. What was his average?

57. Ray Grimes became the Cubs starting first baseman in what year?

58. What was his batting average that season?

59. What was his first name?

60. What was his nickname?

61. On April 26 and April 27, 1922, what did Grimes do?

62. During that season, he had an RBI in how many consecutive games?

63. What was Grime's batting average in 1922?

64. How many doubles did he have that season?

65. After suffering a slipped disc in June of 1923, Grime's career would end prematurely. What was his lifetime batting average?

66. How tall was Earl Adams?

67. What was his nickname?

68. Who gave him the nickname?

69. In what year did Adams lead the league in putouts, assists, and fielding average?

Chicago Cubs Facts & Trivia

70. What was his batting average in 1926?

71. Adams also did what, in the first inning against the Phillies on August 24, 1927?

72. How many errors did George Grantham make in 1923?

73. How many did he make the following year?

74. What position did he play?

75. What was his nickname?

76. Cliff Heathcote was traded by the Cardinals to the Cubs between games of a doubleheader, on Memorial Day of 1922. How many hits did he get in that second game?

77. In what year did he lead the league in fielding average?

78. Heathcote had one at bat in a World Series. What did he do?

79. Arnold Statz had his best season for the Cubs in 1923. What was his average?

80. How many hits did he have that year?

81. How many seasons did "Rabbit" Maranville play with the Cubs?

82. What happened on July 6, 1925?

83. This former Cub manager had the nickname "Moon." Who was he?

84. What is he known for?

85. What manager did "Moon" replace?

86. What was "Moon's" record as Cub manager?

6
THE JOE MCCARTHY ERA

On October 13, 1925, Joe McCarthy was named the new Cubs manager. He had quite a challenge in front of him. The Cubs had been on a downslide and there were many holes to plug. But McCarthy went to work and the era became one of the most exciting and productive in team history.

The first thing McCarthy did was to pluck "Hack" Wilson from the Giants farm chain. Other players who blossomed under McCarthy were pitchers Charlie Root and Guy Bush, along with catcher Gabby Hartnett and outfielder Riggs Stephenson. Some players didn't last under the tight reign of McCarthy. Grover Alexander was waived to the Cardinals in June, 1926, after failing to adhere to the new training rules.

But for the most part, the Cubs adapted and their play improved. The 1926 team finished 4th as did the 1927 Cubs. But again, their brand of baseball was exciting, and the fans responded. 1927 marked the first time in history that a National League team drew over one million fans. That year, 1,163,347 fans flocked to Wrigley Field.

With the additions of pitcher Pat Malone and outfielder Kiki Cuyler, the 1928 team crept to third place, only four games behind league champ St. Louis. In that off season, Chicago acquired the great Rogers Hornsby from the Boston Braves. Even though his prime years were behind him, Hornsby seemed to be the spark the Cubs needed as they routed the Pirates to win the National League pennant by 10½ games. As a team, Chicago hit .303 and smashed 140 home runs. However, the Cubs were beaten handily in five games in the World Series by the Philadelphia Athletics. That loss led owner William Wrigley to fire McCarthy at the close of the 1930 when the Cubs finished second. His successor was Hornsby, who proved to be a poor handler of his players, most notably Hack Wilson. The 1931 team finished third and it was very evident that once again, the Cubs needed a spark.

SOME STARS OF THE ERA

Joe McCarthy

Despite winning only one pennant with the Cubs, Joe McCarthy had an outstanding managerial career, winning nine pennants and seven World Series in 24 years. Another amazing note was that his teams never finished in the second division.

Although possessing great knowledge of the game, McCarthy never played in the Major Leagues. He became a player-manager in the minor leagues at the age of 26 with Wilkes-Barre in 1913. That season he also hit .325, and his team finished in 2nd place. Buffalo purchased his contract and won the pennant in 1915. Buffalo sold off a lot of their stars. McCarthy was offered to the Yankees, but they didn't pay the $3,000 asking price.

For the next 10 years, McCarthy remained with Louisville where he took over as manager in 1919. It was in Louisville that he developed outfielder Earle Combs, whom the Yankees purchased for $65,000, quite a sum of money in those days. Then his chance came with the Cubs and with it his first success.

Unfortunately, he was wrongly blamed by William Wrigley for the loss to the Athletics in the 1929 Series. Given his career success, one can only wonder what he might have accomplished if given the opportunity to manage the Cubs for a few more years.

Trivia Questions

1. Where was McCarthy born?

2. The Cubs finished 4th in 1926. What was their record?

3. Chicago was leading 8-0 in game four of the 1929 World Series against the Athletics. What happened in the 7th inning of that game?

4. What was the final score of that game?

5. What was McCarthy's record with the Cubs?

6. After he left the Cubs, what team signed him to be its manager?

7. How many pennants did he win for that team?

8. How many World Series did he win for them?

9. What other Major League team did he manage?

10. In what year was he elected to the Hall of Fame?

Rogers Hornsby

On November 7, 1928, Rogers Hornsby was dealt by the Boston Braves to the Cubs. It cost Chicago a lot, but owner William Wrigley could afford it. Wrigley gave the Braves five players, plus $200,000 for the "Rajah." He proved his worth the next season by hitting .380 with 39 home runs and 149 runs batted in to lead the Cubs to the pennant. However, in

1930, he broke an ankle and played in just 42 games, batting .308. Since the Cubs finished just two games behind the pennant winning Cardinals, one could assume that had he been healthy, Chicago might have won a second pennant and Joe McCarthy may not have been fired as manager. But that was not the case. When McCarthy was fired, Hornsby took over as manager and won the final four games of the 1930 season.

As a manager, Hornsby was a study in contrasts. As the greatest right-handed hittter of all time, he expected nothing but perfection. But even though he didn't want his players smoking and drinking, Hornsby spent a lot of his free time at the racetrack. Later, there were investigations into his gambling habits, but no charges were made.

Hornsby managed and played into the 1932 season, but mostly just managed. Then, as relations with the front office continued to diminish, he was fired on August 2 of that year. He rejoined the Cardinals in 1933, then spent four seasons as player-manager of the St. Louis Browns. He did return to the Cubs in 1958 and helped develop a couple of superstars in Ron Santo and Billy Williams.

Hornsby was elected to the Hall of Fame in 1942.

Trivia Questions

1. Where was Hornsby born?

2. Over a five-year period with the Cardinals from 1921 thru 1925, what was Hornsby's average?

3. After leaving the Cardinals, what team did he go to?

4. How many hits did Hornsby have with the Cubs in 1929?

5. How many runs did he score that season?

Chicago Cubs Facts & Trivia

6. What feat did Hornsby accomplish on April 24, 1931?

7. How many runs did he drive in that game?

8. Who replaced Hornsby as Cubs manager?

9. What was Hornsby's lifetime batting average?

10. In what year was he elected to the Hall of Fame?

Hack Wilson

Wilson was one of the most feared hitters of all time along with being one of the most colorful players of any era. He showed both tendencies during his six years with the Cubs. From 1926 thru 1931, Wilson averaged over 30 home runs and 128 RBIs a season. His greatest season came in 1930 when he hit 56 home runs, still a National League record and drove in 190 runs, which is still a Major League record. He did it by swinging a long, thin-handled, 41-ounce bat, just like a toothpick.

Hack got started in life the hard way, as an illegitimate child, born in the mining town of Elwood City, Pennsylvania. He worked various jobs after quitting school in the 6th grade. He liked baseball and played with a mining team. At first Hack was a catcher, but he broke his leg in his first game in the Blue Ridge League in 1921 and afterwards moved to the outfield. A few years later he was signed by the New York Giants. After playing briefly with the Giants, Wilson was sent back to Toledo where he was plucked off the roster in the draft after the 1925 season by new Cubs manager Joe McCarthy.

Wilson was a heavy drinker, but he was able to produce on the diamond. McCarthy gave him some rope, but after Joe was replaced as manager by Rogers Hornsby, Wilson's days as a Cub were coming to a close. He was traded to St. Louis, and from there, he went to the Dodgers. Finally, Hack's career came to a close in 1934 with the Phillies.

After his playing days were over, Wilson had a number of low paying jobs and died broke at the age of 48. Hack was finally elected to the Hall of Fame by the Veterans Committee in 1979.

Trivia Questions

1. How much did the Cubs pay for Wilson?

2. How many home runs did he hit as a Cub?

3. How many homers did he hit in his career?

4. How many home runs did Hack hit in 1929?

5. How many runs did he drive in that season?

6. In the 7th inning of the 4th game of the 1929 World Series, Hack misplayed two fly balls against the Athletics. Who hit the first one?

7. While with Chicago, Wilson was offered $15,000 to fight the first baseman from the White Sox. Who was he?

8. How many grand slams did Hack hit in the 1930 season?

9. How many lifetime hits did he have?

10. What was Wilson's lifetime batting average?

Chicago Cubs Facts & Trivia

More Questions About This Era

1. Which team did Charlie Root break into the Majors with?

2. What was his record with that team?

3. How many games did Root win with the Cubs?

4. What was his Major League record?

5. What were the most games he won in a season?

6. What was Root's nickname?

7. Root gave up two home runs to Babe Ruth in the 3rd game of the 1932 World Series. The 2nd one was the debated "Called Shot." In what inning did that famous home run occur?

8. How old was he when he won his 200th game?

9. Who did he beat for that win?

10. What was the score of the game?

11. How many minor league games did Root win?

12. How old was he when he retired from the minors?

13. Guy Bush was the only Cub pitcher to win a game in the 1929 World Series against Philadelphia. What was the score?

14. Bush won 20 games in a season only once. In what year did he do that?

15. What was his record as a Cub?

16. What did Bush do on May 25, 1935, while pitching against the Boston Braves?

17. Riggs Stephenson has the highest Cubs lifetime batting average. What is it?

18. What was his highest average in a single season?

19. Stephenson started out in the Majors at second base but was switched to what position?

20. How many years did he lead the league in doubles?

21. What was his nickname in the Major Leagues?

22. On May 30, 1927, this Cub executed an unassisted triple play. Name him.

23. What position did he play?

24. Who hit into the triple play?

25. Who is the only active Cub player to ever die during a season?

26. What was Woody English's highest batting averge with the Cubs?

27. What were the most hits he ever had in a season?

28. What were the most runs English ever scored in a year?

29. Over a three-year period from 1929 thru 1931, how many runs did he score?

Chicago Cubs Facts & Trivia

30. English roomed with what famous Cub?

31. In 1929, this Cubs pitcher was 22-10 and led the National League in strikeouts with 166. Who was he?

32. What was his lifetime record with Chicago?

33. What was Kiki Cuyler's first name?

34. What Major League team did he break in with?

35. From 1928 thru 1930, Cuyler led the league in what category?

36. What was his batting average in 1929?

37. How many runs batted in did he have that season?

38. How many hits did Cuyler have in 1930?

39. How many doubles did he have that season?

40. What was Cuyler's lifetime batting average?

41. How many hits did he have?

42. How many home runs did he hit?

43. How many stolen bases did Kiki have?

44. How old was he when he died?

45. When was Cuyler elected to the Hall of Fame?

7
REBUILDING AND SUCCESS

On August 2, 1932, Charlie Grimm replaced Rogers Hornsby as the Cubs manager. Their styles of managing was as different as night and day. Where Hornsby was a disciplinarian, Grimm was more laid back. As a result, Grimm was more popular with the players, and they showed it on the field. From being out of the pennant race in early August, Chicago won 37 of its last 57 games to win the league crown.

The next stop was the World Series against the New York Yankees, but the Yankees, led by former Cubs skipper Joe McCarthy, routed the Cubs in four-straight games. It was sweet revenge for McCarthy.

The next two seasons were part of a rebuilding process for the Cubs, and they finished 3rd both years. But Chicago added some players who would once again make the team a contender. Players like third baseman Stan Hack, first baseman Phil Cavarretta, outfielders Frank Demaree and Augie Galan along with pitchers Bill Lee, Larry French, and Tex Carleton were added to the roster, and they turned the Cubs around. In 1935, Chicago won the pennant, but once again the Cubs lost the World Series, this time to the Tigers in six games. In 1936, the Cubs finished in a tie for 2nd, followed by another 2nd place finish in 1937. But in 1938, after Grimm resigned as manager and was succeeded by Gabby Hartnett, Chicago took off again and streaked past the Pirates to win its third pennant of the decade. However, Joe McCarthy's Yankees, swept the Cubs again in four straight. The next year Chicago faded to 4th, then in 1940, dropped to 5th with its first losing season in 15 years. After that season, Hartnett was fired, and the Cubs started all over again.

SOME STARS OF THAT ERA

Gabby Hartnett

Charles Leo "Gabby" Hartnett was not only one of the best catchers of all time, he was also a great hitter and a very colorful player. Hartnett reportedly got his nickname from the sports editor of the Chicago *Herald Examiner*, not for talking too much, but for staying silent on a train trip to California.

Hartnett broke into the Majors with the Cubs in 1922, and although he hit just .194, he managed to hang on. The next season he upped his average to .268, then took over as the Cubs catcher. When that happened, Gabby's hitting improved and he became one of the leagues better clutch hitters. His biggest clutch hit came near the end of his career, when he homered in the bottom of the 9th inning as dusk began to fall at Wrigley Field, to beat the Pirates, 6-5. The date was September 28, 1938, and just four days remained in the regular season. The home run gave the Cubs a half game lead over the Pirates, which they held to win the pennant. Gabby's hit became known as the "The Homer in the Gloamin'."

Although he was behind the plate when Babe Ruth hit is disputed "Called Shot" in the 1932 World Series and again when Carl Hubbell struck out five straight batters in the 1934 All-Star Game, that home run against the Pirates has been recorded as one of the most important events in Cub history.

After being fired as Cub manager following the 1940 season, Gabby finished his Major League career with the Giants in 1941. He was elected to the Hall of Fame in 1955.

Chicago Cubs Facts & Trivia

Trivia Questions

1. Hartnett's first Major League hit was what?

2. How many home runs did he have in 1930?

3. How many runs did he drive in that season?

4. In what year did Hartnett win the Most Valuable Player award?

5. What was his batting average that year?

6. Gabby's highest average came in 1937. What was it?

7. In 1965, Hartnett returned to coach in the Majors for one season. What team did he coach for?

8. What was his lifetime batting average?

9. How many times did he catch over 100 games in a season?

10. Of Gabby's 236 career home runs, how many were hit with the Cubs?

Charlie Grimm

    Not only was Grimm a great clutch hitter, he was an even better fielder. He broke into the Majors at the ripe old age of 17 with the Philadelphia Athletics in 1916. He then moved on to the Cardinals, then to the Pirates in late 1919.
    While his fielding was always good, if not spetacular, his hitting wasn't. But Grimm improved at the plate while with Pittsburgh. He would have stayed longer, but his love for beer,

German food, singing and playing the banjo, eventually got on the nerves of owner Barney Dreyfuss. On October 27, 1924, Grimm and teammates Rabbit Maranville and Wilbur Cooper were traded to the Cubs for Vic Aldridge, George Grantham, and Al Niehaus.

Charlie starred with the Cubs, and on August 3, 1932, he became Chicago's player-manager. Of course, you know what happened. The Cubs went on a roll and won the pennant, only to lose to the Yankees in the World Series. The following year, Grimm managed more and played less. After the 1936 season, Charlie retired as a player, and the next season he led the Cubs to a 2nd place finish. In the middle of 1938, Grimm was replaced by Gabby Hartnett.

Charlie then went to the radio booth for Cubs and White Sox games in 1939 and 1940, before returning to coach the Milwaukee Brewers of the American Association in 1941. Then on May 7, 1944, Grimm came back for his second stint with the Cubs and led them to the pennant the following season. In June of 1949, Charlie was replaced by Frankie Frisch, and Grimm went to the front office for the rest of the season. After managing for several seasons again in the minor leagues, Grimm made it up to the big time as manager for a third time to lead the Milwaukee Braves. Charlie didn't have a chance to see just how good his team was going to be, because he was fired in June 1956. The Braves went on to be a National League powerhouse for the rest of the decade, winning the 1957 World Series over the Yankees, losing to New York in 1958, then losing a third-straight National League pennant in a playoff with the Dodgers in 1959.

However, Grimm's career with the Cubs didn't end, for he returned as an executive vice-president and even was field manager for a while in 1960, before going once again to the radio booth. Then in 1961, he was back as a coach.

Grimm died in Arizona at the age of 85 in 1983.

Chicago Cubs Facts & Trivia

Trivia Questions

1. What did Grimm hit in his first Major League season?

2. In 1920, he led the National League first baseman in fielding percentage. What was it?

3. What was his average in 1923?

4. How many hits did he have that season?

5. What was Grimm's batting average in the 1932 World Series?

6. Who took over his first base spot in 1935?

7. How many times did he lead the league in fielding average?

8. How many lifetime hits did he have?

9. How many double plays did he have as a first baseman?

10. What was Grimm's lifetime batting average?

Billy Herman

Herman broke into the Major Leagues with the Cubs after spending five successful seasons in the minors. He was by-passed by the Yankees and picked up by the Cubs for $50,000 in 1931. He finished out that season with Chicago and in 25 games hit .327.

In 1932, as a starter in place of Rogers Hornsby, Billy hit .314 and was on his way to becoming one of the stars of the National League. He was also a great second baseman and in

1933 had 466 putouts, including 16 in a doubleheader against the Phillies.

Billy continued to star with the Cubs, collecting 200 hits a year and hitting .300 numerous times before he moved on to the Brooklyn Dodgers during the 1941 season. Billy had a hard time getting a long with Leo Durocher but still hit well.

Following the 1943 season, he was drafted and entered the Navy. After two years serving in the Pacific, Herman returned to the Dodgers, but by that time he had lost his job to Eddie Stanky. He was also nearing the end of his career and after a brief stint with the Boston Braves, was hired to manage the Pittsburgh Pirates in 1947. But he only managed the Pirates for one season, in which they finished last. After bouncing around the minors for a number of years, Herman was named to manage the Boston Red Sox. But he was out after two disappointing 9th place finishes. However, Billy did get some satisfaction when he was elected to the Hall of Fame in 1975.

Trivia Questions

1. What was Herman's full name?

2. How many hits did he have in 1932?

3. Billy exceeded 900 total chances in a season at second base, how many seasons?

4. What were two of his nicknames?

5. How many doubles did he have in each of the 1935 and 1936 seaons?

6. How many hits did he have in 1935?

7. What was Herman's batting average that year?

Chicago Cubs Facts & Trivia

8. In his first game as a Dodger, how many hits did he get?

9. How many hits did he have in his career?

10. What was his lifetime batting average?

More Questions About That Era

1. Who led the Cubs in home runs in 1932?

2. How many homers did he hit that season?

3. What was pitcher Lon Warneke's nickname?

4. He led the league in victories in 1932. How many did he have?

5. What was his earned run average that season?

6. How many games did Warneke win during the 1935 World Series?

7. What did he do after his Major League career came to an end?

8. What was Frank Demaree's batting average in 1933?

9. Who was he filling in for?

10. How many hits did Demaree have in 1936?

11. This shortstop played opposite Billy Herman in the 1930s. Who was he?

12. This same player also took over as manager of what

team midway through the 1959 season?

13. How many years did Babe Herman play with the Cubs?

14. How many home runs did Chuck Klein hit in his first season with the Cubs?

15. What team did the Cubs get him from?

16. Pitcher Bill Lee was sold by the Cardinals to the Cubs. How much did Chicago pay for him?

17. What did Lee do in his first two Major League starts?

18. What was his record in his rookie season of 1934?

19. What was his record the next season?

20. Late in 1935, the Cubs had a 21-game winning streak. How many of those games did Lee win?

21. His best overall season came in 1938. What was Lee's record?

22. What was his earned run average that year?

23. How many shutouts did he have?

24. What was his won-loss record as a Cub?

25. In 1935, Augie Galan batted 646 times without doing what?

26. As a switch hitter, Galan became the first player to do what?

27. How many hits did he have in 1935?

28. What was Galan's nickname?

29. Lefthanded pitcher Larry French won 197 games in his career. How many wins came as a Cub?

30. How many shutouts did he have as a Cub?

31. What was "Ripper" Collins's first name?

32. What position did he play?

33. What happened to Collins on June 29, 1937?

34. How much did the Cubs pay for Dizzy Dean?

35. What was his record for the 1938 Cubs?

36. What was his overall record with Chicago?

37. In what year did Hank Leiber join the Cubs?

38. What position did he play?

39. What was his lifetime batting average?

40. How many years did he play with Chicago?

41. How many years did Dick Bartell play with the Cubs?

42. As a shortstop, how many errors did he make in the 1939 season?

8
THE WAR-TIME CUBS

The early 1940s were a tough time for the Cubs and Major League Baseball. Because of the war, many players were either drafted or enlisted in the armed forces. Chicago lost its share of players, and the early '40s were difficult years.

The Cubs had new men at the top. Jimmy Wilson was the field manager, and James Gallagher took over the front office as general manager. Together, they made a number of deals, when combined with the players already lost to "Uncle Sam," would drag the team down to the bottom of the National League. Billy Herman was traded away, as were Larry French and Augie Galan. In 1941, Chicago finished 6th and followed that up with another 6th place finish in 1942. The following year, the Cubs moved up to 5th and in 1944 inched into 4th place. But still, they weren't even close as a favorite to win the pennant in 1945.

The Cardinals had already won three-straight pennants and a couple of championships and were favored to win the NL pennant again. The Cubs started off slowly that year but took the lead on July 8. It was a dog-fight between Chicago and St. Louis the rest of the way, but the Cubs prevailed, clinching the pennant on September 29. When it was over, Chicago had finished three games ahead of St. Louis.

But once again, the Cubs were unable to win the World Series. They battled the Tigers for seven games but still lost. This was the closest the Cubs had come to winning it all since

1908.

1945 also marked the end of the war, so players would be returning to the Majors in droves. However, no one really knew, what their impact would be. But it was hoped that quality baseball would be back the next season.

SOME PLAYERS OF THAT ERA

Stan Hack

Hack was one of the Cubs all-time great players and spent his entire 16 year career in the Windy City. From 1932 thru 1947, he was a fixture at third base. He was not known as a power hitter, but he sprayed enough hits around to finish with a .301 lifetime batting average and nearly 2,200 hits.

His career in the big time started out slowly as Stan hit just .236 in his first season in Chicago. After a little seasoning in the minors, he hit .311 in the pennant winning season of 1935. By then, he was a team leader, not only as a hitter but as a fielder. Twice he led the league's third basemen in fielding average, twice he led in assists, and five times, Stan led in putouts.

Hack was always tough in the clutch. In the 1938 World Series, he hit .471 against the Yankees, and in the 1945 Series against the Tigers, Stan hit .367. His biggest hit in that Series was a smash into the twilight to left field that hit a sprinkler faucet in front of Hank Greenburg, driving in the winning run. The ball bounced over Greenburg's head, and scorers deliberated several hours before ruling it a hit and not an error.

After the 1943 season, Stan retired. His relationship with manager Jimmy Wilson had soured to the point where Hack wanted out. But his retirement last only a few months because Wilson was fired the following May and Hack was talked into returning to the team in mid-June. The following year of 1945, Stan hit .323, the highest in his career.

Chicago Cubs Facts & Trivia

However, the end was approaching. In 1946, he played less at third base. He was approaching 37, and he suffered a broken hand. He retired following the 1947 season after playing just part time. He then managed in the minor leagues for several seasons before returning to the Cubs to take over as skipper. His club lacked talent though and after three seasons, he was fired.

After coaching with the Cardinals for two seasons, in which he also served briefly as interim manager, Stan was back in the minors managing. He then left baseball in 1966.

Trivia Questions

1. Where did Stan break into the minors at?

2. What was his nickname?

3. From 1936 thru 1941, he tied a National League record for doing what?

4. When did Stan collect his 2,000th Major League hit?

5. What was it?

6. What pitcher did it come against?

7. What were the most home runs he ever hit in a season?

8. What was his best finish in his three seasons as manager of the Cubs?

9. How many lifetime hits did he have?

10. What was his lifetime average?

Phil Cavarretta

If ever there was a player born to play baseball and to become a Cub, it was Phil Cavarretta. Not only was he born in Chicago, he also played in that city his entire career.

Cavy played briefly with two minor league teams in 1934 before being called up by the Cubs on September 25 of that year at the age of only 18! In his first game, he homered to give the Cubs a 1-0 victory over the Reds. Cavarretta finished out the season and in seven games hit .381. The next year, he nailed down the first base job and had a solid year with a .275 average, eight home runs, and 62 RBIs. He continued to hustle and play well and was named team captain following the 1943 season.

In 1945, Cavy led the Cubs to the pennant, winning the batting championship with a .355 average along with winning the Most Valuable Player award. He also had a great Series, hitting .423, but the Cubs lost to the Tigers.

The following season he was moved to the outfield, but a few years later returned to first base. He continued to give each game his best. Then on July 21, 1951, Cavy was named the Cubs manager. The next day he drove in seven runs in a doubleheader-sweep of the Phillies. The last four came in on Cavy's pinch-hit, grand slam homer. But even those heroics couldn't keep the Cubs from finishing last that season.

The following year they finished 5th, then in 1953 fell to 7th. In spring training of 1954, Cavy made the mistake of telling owner P. K. Wrigley that the team probably wouldn't do very well that season. For that honesty, he found himself looking for work. He found it later that summer when the White Sox signed him as a utility player. He hit .316 and hit a grand slam home run to help beat the Red Sox on August 3. However, after going 0-4 early in the 1955 season, Cavy was released as a player.

After his playing days were over, he managed in the minors for a while, then coached for the Tigers before serving as a coach and minor league instructor with the Mets.

Trivia Questions

1. Manager Charlie Grimm had his own nickname for Cavarretta. What was it?

2. How many triples did he hit in 1935?

3. How many hits did Cavarretta have in 1943?

4. In 1944, he hit over .300 for a full season. What was his average?

5. How many games did he play in?

6. How many runs did he drive in that year?

7. How many runs did Cavy drive in, in 1945?

8. What was his uniform number?

9. How many lifetime hits did he have?

10. What was his lifetime batting average?

Claude Passeau

Passeau spent nine of his 13 big league seasons with the Cubs, and despite numerous injuries, he was a very productive right-handed pitcher.

After getting a college degree in 1932, Claude became a fireman on a merchant marine ship. After sailing the world, he decided he would attempt to become a baseball player. He bounced around the minors before he was picked up by the

Pirates after winning 20 games at Des Moines in 1935.

He was soon shipped off to the Phillies, and from 1936 thru 1938, his record was 36-51. However, despite his losing record, Passeau pitched well and was among the National League leaders in innings pitched and strikeouts.

On May 29, 1939, he was traded to the Cubs for three players. The following year Passeau won 20 games. In the pennant winning season of 1945, he was 17-9, and despite a sore arm, he shut out the Tigers in game three of the World Series. In 1946, Claude slipped to 9-8, but he was just 2-6 the following year after having spinal surgery. In late September of 1947, Passeau was released.

After that, Claude went back home to his farm and was later elected county sheriff.

Trivia Questions

1. What was Claude's lifetime Major League record?

2. What was his record with the Cubs?

3. From September 21, 1941 to May 20, 1946, Passeau did what?

4. What was his nickname?

5. Passeau was traded from the Phillies to the Cubs for three players. Name them.

6. What college did he go to?

7. What was his major?

8. Besides beating the Dodgers, 14-1, on May 19, 1941, Passeau also did what in that game?

9. Where was he born?

10. How many lifetime home runs did he hit?

More Questions About The War-Time Cubs

1. How many seasons did Jimmy Wilson manage the Cubs?

2. After winning their 1944 opener, the Cubs went on a long losing streak and Wilson resigned. How many games did they lose before he quit?

3. What was his best finish?

4. What number did Claude Passeau wear?

5. How many consecutive years did Bill Nicholson lead the Cubs in home runs?

6. He lost the Most Valuable Player award in 1944 to the Cardinals Marty Marion. What was the vote?

7. How many home runs did Nicholson hit that season?

8. That year he tied a Major League record by leading the league in homers and runs batted in for two consecutive seasons? Which two players did he share that mark with?

9. What Major League team did Nicholson break in with?

10. What college did he go to?

11. What team did the Cubs trade Nicholson to?

12. How many home runs did Nicholson hit as a Cub?

13. How many of those homers were grand slams?

14. What were some of Dom Dallessandro's nicknames?

15. How tall was he?

16. Dom was once traded for this star. Who was he?

17. Of his 22 career home runs, how many were grand slams?

18. This pitcher struck out pinch-hitter Tommy O'Brien to clinch the 1945 pennant for the Cubs. Name him.

19. What Cub had the nickname of McClint?

20. What position did he play?

21. On September 13, 1942, Cubs shortstop Lennie Merullo did what?

22. How many years did he play with the Cubs?

23. What was Lou Novikoff's nickname?

24. What Hall of Fame was he elected to?

25. What was Cy Block's lifetime batting average?

26. How many Major League games did he play?

27. Pitcher Hiram Bithorn was born in what country?

28. What was his record in his rookie seaon with the Cubs?

29. What was his record in 1943?

30. Bithorn led the league with how many shutouts that season?

31. What was Peanuts Lowrey's first name?

32. He broke in with the Cubs playing what position in 1943?

33. What was his batting average that year?

34. What year did Hank Wyse break into the Majors with the Cubs?

35. What pitcher did he beat to win his first big league game?

36. What was the score?

37. How many games did he win for Chicago in 1945?

38. Don Johnson broke into the Majors at what age?

39. Don led the Cubs in doubles in 1944 with how many?

40. Where was Andy Pafko born?

41. How many runs did he drive in during his first Major League game?

42. How many fans were in attendance for that game?

43. In 1944, Pafko led the league with how many assists?

44. How many RBIs did he have in 1945?

45. How many home runs did he hit in 1950?

46. What team was Pafko traded to in 1951?

47. What was Frank Secory's nickname?

48. After his playing career was over, what did Secory do?

49. What was Hank Borowy's record for the 1945 Cubs?

50. What was his lifetime record as a Cub?

9
THE TOUGH YEARS

Even though a number of Cub veterans returned from the war ready to play, for many their best baseball was behind them.

In 1946, Chicago finished 3rd, then sank to 6th the following season. With the emphasis on a younger team, the 1948 Cubs took their lumps and finished last. Charlie Grimm's days as a manager were numbered, and he was replaced in June 1949 by Frankie Frisch. However, even though Chicago picked up outfielders Hank Sauer and Frankie Baumholtz, Frisch was unable to get the team going, and once again the Cubs came in last. Despite belting 161 home runs in 1950, Chicago finished 7th with an infield that led both leagues with 201 errors! In the 1951 season, Phil Cavarretta replaced Frisch as manager, but the Cubs once again finished as a last place team. Plus, slugger Andy Pafko was traded during the season with three teammates. Besides losing a slugger, the players received from the Dodgers never produced. The 1952 team surprised everyone by finishing 5th. The Cubs were able to get good performances from rookie first baseman Dee Fondy and second year third baseman Ransom Jackson. Hank Sauer won the Most Valuable Player award as the club finished at .500. But in 1953, the Chicago reverted to the past and dropped to 7th. The Cubs' troubles would continue a while longer.

SOME PLAYERS FROM THAT ERA

Bob Rush

During a period of futility for the Cubs, Bob Rush pitched as well as anyone could under the circumstances. He broke into the Majors in 1948 and had a disappointing 5-11 season. In 1952, Rush won 17 games, but if he'd had any support, he could have won a lot more. He lost two 1-0 games, two 2-0 games, one 3-0, and five others by just one run.

Rush made the All-Star Team that year and ended up the winning pitcher when his teammate Hank Sauer hit a two-run homer for a rain shortened 2-1 win.

He was traded from a team going nowhere to the World Champion Milwaukee Braves in December 1957, and in 1958, he went 10-6. He pitched for the Braves until the middle of the 1960 season.

Trivia Questions

1. Where was Bob born?

2. What was his middle name?

3. What was his record as a Cub pitcher?

4. After leaving the Braves, what Major League team did Rush finish up with?

5. What was his Major League record?

Hank Sauer

Sauer was drafted by the Reds in 1940, but the road to the Majors was a long one for him. It took Hank 11 years before he was able to stay for good, but once he did, Sauer made up for lost time.

In 1948, Sauer blasted 35 home runs for Cincinnati, which set a team record. The following season, he started slowly, then was traded to the Cubs. It was a trade that Chicago would not complain about.

In 1952, Sauer hit 37 homers, which tied him with Ralph Kiner for the league lead. His 121 runs batted in led the Majors as he helped the Cubs to a 5th place finish. In 1954, Sauer upped his home run total to a career high 41. Then in the spring of 1956, he was traded to the Cardinals. It was a trade that most couldn't understand. But Sauer had turned 37, and after spending a year in St. Louis, he finished up with the New York and San Francisco Giants. He then became a scout and a batting instructor with the Giants farm system.

Trivia Questions

1. What was Sauer's nickname while with the Cubs?

2. In the trade that sent Sauer to the Cubs, they also received Frankie Baumholtz. What players did the Cubs trade to the Reds?

3. How many home runs did Sauer hit in his seven years with the Cubs?

4. How many runs did he drive in?

5. How many times as a Cub did he hit three homers in a game?

6. The Cubs traded Sauer to the Cardinals for what player?

7. What was his number?

8. What was his Major League lifetime batting average?

9. How many home runs did he hit?

10. How many runs did he drive in?

Ralph Kiner

Kiner's most productive seasons came with Pittsburgh. At the age of 30, he was traded by the Pirates to the Cubs on June 4, 1953. Cub fans should have been excited about the power possibilities of Kiner and Hank Sauer. But both men played left field, and both were just average. Someone had to move, and Sauer, who was the fans favorite, agreed to play right field. Kiner had a good first season with Chicago, hitting 28 homers as a Cub and 35 overall. But the next season he suffered from the effects of a bad back and hit only 22 dingers. With his $90,000 salary, the Cubs found it hard to justify keeping him, so he was traded to the Indians in November 1954. He played just one season with the Indians, hitting 18 home runs, then he retired.

Trivia Questions

1. How many players were involved in the trade that sent Kiner to the Cubs?

2. In addition to the player the Cubs sent the Pirates, how much money did they give?

3. When Kiner was traded to Cleveland, who did the Cubs receive?

4. How many homers did Kiner hit in his career?

Chicago Cubs Facts & Trivia

5. In what year was he voted in the Hall of Fame?

More Questions About That Era

1. Johnny Schmitz made his first appearance in the Majors with the Cubs in 1941. He came in as a reliever and threw one pitch. Who did he get out?

2. How did he end up winning that game?

3. In 1946, he led the National League in strikeouts with how many?

4. What was his record that year?

5. How many complete games did Schmitz have in 1948?

6. What was his nickname?

7. He also was called the "Dodger Killer". How many lifetime wins did he have against them?

8. What did Eddie Waitkus hit for the Cubs in 1946?

9. In what year did Bob Sheffing become Cub manager?

10. What position did Hal Jeffcoat play?

11. He later switched to what position?

12. What position did Roy Smalley play?

13. How many errors did he make in 1950?

14. He also led the league in putouts that season with how

many?

15. How many home runs did he have that year?

16. On June 28, 1950, Smalley accomplished what?

17. What was pitcher Warren Hacker's lifetime record with the Cubs?

18. His best year came in 1952. What was his record?

19. How many shutouts did he have that season?

20. What was Frankie Frisch's managerial record with the Cubs?

21. What was the batting average of Frankie Baumholtz in 1952?

22. How tall was pitcher Paul Minner?

23. What team was he most successful against?

24. What position did Randy Jackson play?

25. How many home runs did he hit in 1955?

26. What team did the Cubs trade him to?

27. Of his 103 lifetime homers, how many came with the Cubs?

28. How many games did Chuck Connors play with the Cubs?

29. In what year?

Chicago Cubs Facts & Trivia

30. What was his batting average?

31. How many home runs did he hit?

32. What did Connors quit baseball to go into?

33. What did Dee Fondy do in his first Major League at bat?

34. What was his batting average in 1953?

35. How many hits did he have that season?

36. How many stolen bases did Fondy have in 1954?

37. What team did the Cubs trade him to?

38. What number did Paul Schramka wear?

39. How many games did he play with the Cubs?

40. How many times did he bat?

10
THE MAKING OF A SLUGGER

In 1954, during spring training, manager Phil Cavarretta was fired after telling Phil Wrigley the team would probably have a lousy year. Stan Hack was brought in to replace Cavarretta, but the Cubs could do no better than 7th place.

However, a young shortstop by the name of Ernie Banks became a regular that season. The following year the Cubs finished 6th, then dropped all the way to the basement in 1956. It was Chicago's 10th consecutive second-division finish.

After the '56 season, Bob Scheffing replaced Hack as manager, and the Cubs finished tied for 7th place. With Banks leading the way in 1958, the Cubs belted a team record 182 home runs and moved up to 5th place. Besides Banks, Walt Moryn, Lee Walls, Dale Long, and Bobby Thompson, all hit 20 or more homers that season. The Cubs scored 709 runs in the process.

In 1959, Chicago tied for 5th place for the second consecutive season, even though Banks continued to blister opposing pitchers. The problem was that the Cubs pitching staff, with the exception of Glen Hobbie who won 16 games, wasn't able to contribute much. Sheffing was fired after the '59 season despite a 74-80 record, the team's best in seven years.

Charlie Grimm managed the Cubs for the first 17 games of the 1960 season, then was replaced by Hall-of-Fame shortstop Lou Boudreau. While the "Good Kid" moved to the playing field, Grimm went to the broadcast booth. But Chicago still finished only a game above last place. The Cubs had a lot of serious problems!

MR. CUB AND TEAMMATE

Ernie Banks

Ernie Banks, of course, will always be "Mr. Cub." During his 19 seasons with the Cubs, Ernie hit 512 home runs and gave fans enough thrills to last a lifetime.

He was the second of 12 children and was born in Dallas, Texas. He helped the family out at home, and while going to Booker T. Washington High School in Dallas, he played football, basketball, and softball. While still in high school during the summer of 1948, Ernie began playing shortstop for the Detroit Colts, which were based in Amarillo, Texas. The Colts were strictly a Negro team and played their games in Texas, Oklahoma, New Mexico, Kansas, and Nebraska. For two years, Ernie played with the Colts before signing with the Kansas City Monarchs of the Negro American League after his high school graduation. Ernie was paid $300 a month to play for the Monarchs.

After a two-year stint in the army, Ernie was playing again with the Monarchs when the Cubs purchased his contract on September 8, 1953. On September 14 of that season, Ernie saw Wrigley Field for the first time. In his first game on September 17, he was 0-3 and made an error at short. But, in his third game with the Cubs on September 20, Banks hit his first Major League home run. In 10 games that year, he hit .314.

The following year, in his first full season, Banks hit 19 homers, a team record for a rookie. Then a breakthrough year came in 1955 when Ernie belted 44 homers and drove in 117 runs. Also, "Mr. Cub" belted five grand slams that seaon. His home run total set a Major League record for most homers by a shortstop.

Chicago Cubs Facts & Trivia

In 1958 and 1959, Ernie won back-to-back Most Valuable Player awards. In 1958, he belted a league leading 47 homers, drove in 129 runs, scored 119 times, and hit .313. The following season Ernie smacked 45 home runs, drove in 143 runs, and hit .304. In 1960, the home runs continued to fly off his bat as he led the league for the second and final time in home runs with 41. As his production declined some, Banks was moved around to several different positions. The year was 1961. First Ernie went to left field, then back to short, and finally to first base where he would spend the rest of his career. His hitting returned while settling in at first, and in 1962, he hit 37 homers and drove in 104 runs. But still the Cubs kept losing.

Finally, in 1967, things started to look up for the team. Leo Durocher had become manager of the club the previous season and things were starting to happen. The 1967 Cubs finished 3rd as Ernie belted 23 homers and drove in 95. In the disappointing season of 1969, Banks slumped at the end, but still drove in 106 runs. In 1970, age quickly took its toll on Ernie, who by now was 39 years old. He played in only 72 games that season, but he still hit his 500th home run. It was all over for him after the 1971 season, in which he batted only 83 times.

On February 14, 1977, Ernie was elected to the Baseball Hall of Fame. Even though he never played in a World Series, he achieved more than enough to secure his place in baseball history. "Mr. Cub" will be remembered by Cub fans for all time.

Trivia Questions

1. Who served up Ernie's first Major League home run?

2. What kind of a pitch was it?

3. What was Ernie's average in 1954?

4. On August 4, 1955, he did what?

5. How many times would he do that in his career?

6. Between 1962 and 1969, how many times did Ernie lead the league in assists by first basemen?

7. How many times did he lead in putouts?

8. When did Banks hit his 400th home run?

9. Who did he hit it off?

10. What did he do on June 11, 1966?

11. What was Ernie's lifetime batting average?

12. How many hits did he have?

13. How many extra base hits did he have?

14. How many RBIs did he have?

15. How many doubles did he hit?

16. How many runs did Ernie score?

17. How many triples did he hit?

18. Who served up his 500th homer?

19. On what date did he hit his 511th home run?

20. When did he hit is 512th home run?

21. What team did that home run come against?

22. When did Ernie get his final hit?

23. What was it?

24. What was his lifetime slugging average?

25. How many games did he play?

Gene Baker

Gene Baker and Ernie Banks were the first black players for the Cubs. They came up together near the end of the 1953 season. For Gene, the final promotion to the big time was long overdue. He was 28-years-old and had played for the Kansas City Monarchs of the Negro League before being signed by the Cubs in 1950. He was a dazzling shortstop, but when he made it to the Cubs, he was told Banks would be the shortstop and he would play second base.

In 1957, Baker was moved to third base during spring training, and after playing just 12 games that season was traded to the Pirates. The following year he suffered a serious knee injury and spent the next year and a half on the inactive list. He was released by the Pirates in June of 1961. But he stayed in baseball as the Pirates made him manager of their Class "D" farm club in Batavia, New York. He was the second African-American to manage in organized baseball. Baker later would coach for the Pirates.

Trivia Questions

1. What was Baker's average in 1954?

2. Where was he born?

3. How many years did he play in the Majors?

4. How many hits did he have?

5. What was his lifetime average?

Other Questions About That Era

1. On May 12, 1955, Sam Jones threw a no-hitter against what club?

2. Who was his catcher?

3. What was the score?

4. Jones walked the bases loaded in the top of the 9th and then proceeded to strike out the side. Name the three players he struck out.

5. How many times did Jones lead the league in walks?

6. How many walks did he issue in 1955?

7. Sam was traded by the Cubs to what team?

8. In May of 1955, Cubs outfielder Bob Speake hit how many home runs?

9. How many assists did outfielder Moose Moryn have in 1956?

10. How many home runs did he hit that season?

11. On Memorial Day in 1958, in the second game of a doubleheaer, Moose did what?

12. What team were the Cubs playing?

Chicago Cubs Facts & Trivia

13. How many home runs did Moose hit in 1958?

14. What was Jim Brosnan's won-loss record with the Cubs?

15. What happened to him on June 21, 1957?

16. Name his two best-selling books.

17. How many years did Moe Drabowsky pitch for the Cubs?

18. What was his record with the Cubs?

19. When he was signed to a bonus contract with the Cubs, how much was it worth?

20. Moe tied a Major League record by hitting how many batters in one game?

21. Moe was on the mound against the Cardinals when Stan Musial did what?

22. He set a record in the 1966 World Series as an Oriole by striking out how many Dodgers in a row?

23. On May 26, 1957, Dick Drott struck out 15 Milwaukee Braves. How many times did he fan Hank Aaron?

24. What was his record that season?

25. After developing a sore arm in 1958, what was his record that year?

26. How many appearances did relief pitcher Don Elston make in 1958?

27. How many saves did he have that season?

28. What was his record?

29. What did Lee Walls do on July 2, 1957?

30. Against what team?

31. What was his batting average in 1958?

32. How many home runs did he hit?

33. How many runs did he drive in on April 24, 1958?

34. Against what team?

35. Who was the Cub pitcher that won the game?

36. In what year did Dale Long begin playing for the Cubs?

37. Long was a first baseman, but on August 20, 1958, he played for two outs at what position?

38. On May 13, 1960, second baseman Tony Taylor and catcher Cal Neeman were traded to the Phils for who?

39. Pitcher Glen Hobbie's first Major League win was a shutout. What team did it come against?

40. What was his record in 1959?

41. How many complete games did he have that season?

42. How many losses did he have in 1960?

43. What famous Hall-of-Famer finished out the season as Cubs manager in 1960?

11
THE GREAT EXPERIMENT

In December of 1960, owner P. K. Wrigley announced an innovation for Baseball. Instead of a manager, the Cubs would have a "College of Coaches". Wrigley planned to have eight rotating coaches running the Cubs, beginning in the 1961 season! It made no sense to anyone who knew Baseball and created chaos in the clubhouse.

The original eight coaches were Charlie Grimm, Vedie Himsl, Rip Collins, Harry Craft, Elvin Tappe, Goldie Holt, Rube Walker, and Bobby Adams. Later on, Buck O'Neill, Al Dark, Bob Kennedy, Lou Klein, Charlie Metro, Mel Wright, Freddie Martin, and Mel Harder would join in.

Despite the knowledge of the "College of Coaches", the 1961 Cubs could finish no better than 7th. In the expansion year of 1962, the Cubs finished 9th, ahead of only the New York Mets, which wasn't hard to do because the Mets lost a record 120 games. The other expansion team, the Houston Colt .45s, finished ahead of Chicago, which wasn't that hard to do because the Cubs lost 103 games.

Bob Kennedy was named head coach for 1963, and the Cubs finished in 7th place with a record of 82-80, their best mark in 17 years. But the promise of 1963 vanished in 1964. In February of that year, second baseman Ken Hubbs was killed in a plane crash. Without the stellar fielding second baseman behind it, the pitching went south, and the Cubs sank to 8th.

In mid-June of 1965, Kennedy was fired, and Lou Klein

took the helm. But the Cubs were terrible that year and once again finished 8th. The good news was that the Cubs had some developing young talent who would help to turn the team around a few years later.

A STAR SO BRIGHT, SO SHORT IN LIFE

Ken Hubbs

One of the most tragic stories in the long history of the Cubs is the death of 22-year-old second baseman Ken Hubbs. He and a friend were killed when Hubbs's Cessna 172 crashed shortly after take off into Utah Lake near Provo, Utah. It was Thursday, February 13, 1964, and his death was a shock to the Cubs and the rest of the baseball community.

Hubbs set the National League on fire in his rookie season of 1962. Besides hitting a solid .260, he played a record 78 games at second base without making an error. He handled 418 consecutive chances flawlessly and was named the league's Rookie-of-the-Year. Hubbs was also named to the National League's all-fielding team and became the first rookie to win a Gold Glove Award.

The following year his batting average tailed off to .235, but his fielding remained excellent and the Cubs had high hopes for him. But those dreams vanished with his death.

Trivia Questions

1. In what year did Hubbs sign with the Cubs?

2. When did his 78-game errorless streak begin?

3. When did the streak end?

4. Who were the Cubs playing?

Chicago Cubs Facts & Trivia

5. What kind of an error was it?

6. Name Hubbs's friend who died in the crash with him.

7. Hubbs received all but one vote for Rookie-of-the-Year. Who received that vote?

8. Who won the first Ken Hubbs Memorial Award?

9. How many Major League hits did Hubbs have?

10. What was his lifetime batting average?

More Questions About That Era

1. When did the Cubs acquire pitcher Don Cardwell?

2. What did he do in his Cub debut?

3. What team was he pitching against?

4. What was the score of the game?

5. What was his record that year with the Cubs?

6. In what year did George Altman break in with Chicago?

7. What was his rookie average?

8. How many home runs did Altman hit in June of 1961?

9. He was selected to his first All-Star game that year. He batted once as a pinch-hitter. What did he do?

10. What was his batting average in 1961?

11. How many homers did he have?

12. How many runs did he drive in that year?

13. What was his batting average in 1962?

14. After the 1962 season, George was involved in a six-man trade. Who was he traded to?

15. Altman came back to the Cubs in 1965 from the Mets. Who did the Cubs trade to get him back?

16. How old was pitcher Dick Ellsworth when he broke into the Majors with the Cubs?

17. Ellsworth won his first Major League game against what team?

18. What was the score?

19. What was Dick's record in 1963?

20. What was his earned run average that year?

21. He became the first Cub left-hander to win 20 games since who and in what year?

22. Ellsworth later pitched for the Boston Red Sox and became the first pitcher in both leagues to do what?

23. How long did Lou Brock play with the Cubs?

24. In his rookie season of 1962, what was his average?

25. What did Lou do on June 17 of that year in a game against the Mets at the Polo Grounds?

Chicago Cubs Facts & Trivia

26. Pitcher Bob Buhl had his best record as a Cub in 1964. What was it?

27. On May 8, 1963, he singled off Pirate's pitcher Alvin McBean to break a streak. What was that streak?

28. As a Cub, what was Larry Jackson's ERA in 1963?

29. How many years did Lindy McDaniel pitch for the Cubs?

30. What style did Ted Abernathy use as a pitcher?

12
THE LIP AT THE HELM

The incredibly outspoken Leo "The Lip" Durocher was hired as head coach of the Cubs on October 25, 1965, and he promptly informed everybody that he was the manager of the Chicago Cubs, not a head coach.

With his hiring, Cubs fans hoped he would turn things around, especially after Leo declared: "This is not a 9th place team." He was right. The Cubs finished last in 1966.

Chicago moved up to 3rd the following season, the highest finish and best record of any Cubs team since 1946. There was some hope in the Windy City. The Cubs had a pretty solid team. Ernie Banks was still playing well enough at first base, and Ron Santo at third base and Billy Williams in left field had already proven themselves. Shortstop Don Kessinger and second baseman Glenn Beckert were still being groomed, but they had convinced enough people that they belonged. Catcher Randy Hundley was picked up from the Giants as was pitcher Bill Hands. Left-handed pitcher Ken Holtzman had a pretty good rookie season in 1966, and of course, the ace of the staff was big right-hander Ferguson Jenkins.

The Cubs started slowly in 1968, and at one point, they were held scoreless in 48 consecutive innings. But then, good things started to happen, and the club finished in 3rd again. That year the Cubs picked up outfielder Jim Hickman and relief pitcher Phil Regan from the Dodgers. Bill Hands also developed that season into a dependable starter. It seemed like the Cubs had a team that could challenge for the pennant, and excitement was high going into the 1969 season. The Cubs got off to a quick start in '69 and held an 8½-game lead in mid-August. But you know the rest of the story. The "Amazin' Mets" caught fire, overtaking the Cubs in September, then pulling away to win their first pennant. The Cubs finished eight games behind New York. It was a shocker for the team, their fans, and everyone else who followed the Cubbies. It was hard to get over.

The 1970 team tied for 2nd, despite belting 179 home runs. In 1971, the team's chemistry was falling apart, and many called for Durocher to be fired, as the Cubs finished in a tie for 3rd. Chicago continued to stumble the following year, and Durocher was finally fired on July 24, 1972, and replaced by Whitey Lockman. At that point in the season, the Cubs were two games above .500. The change in managers seemed to give the team new life, as Chicago climbed to another 2nd place finish.

SOME MEMORABLE MEN OF THAT ERA

Leo Durocher

Durocher had one of the most colorful baseball careers of all time. He broke in with the New York Yankees and roomed with the immortal Babe Ruth. He was captain of the 1934 St. Louis Cardinals known as the "Gashouse Gang". He also managed the Brooklyn Dodgers before moving over to skipper the rival New York Giants, where he helped develop a young centerfielder by the name of Willie Mays.

He had done it all and proven he was a winner, but there was still a huge challenge ahead when Leo "The Lip" was hired to take over the Cubs. Durocher was still as brash as ever, but he knew baseball and gave the team, especially the young Cubs, a shot of confidence in their collective arm.

If there ever was a season when the Cubs were expected to

win the pennant, it was that fateful year of 1969. But in the end, not even Leo Durocher could lead the team to the World Series. Durocher received most of the blame. Critics said he didn't rest his players enough, especially during the hot days of July and August. It was really a combination of the Cubs slumping and the Mets continuing to win. But whatever the reasons, it was one of the most disappointing seasons in the team's history.

Eventually, Leo got under the skin of his veteran players, and there were calls for his removal. Owner Philip Wrigley supported Durocher, but finally Leo was replaced. However, Durocher wasn't out of the game for long, because a month after leaving the Cubs, "The Lip" was managing the Houston Astros. However, his personality and mouth got him into trouble there, and he resigned from the job October 1, 1973.

Despite being a mediocre hitter in the majors and having a tendency to infuriate most people, Duroucher was a great manager and student of the game of baseball. He received his biggest honor when he was elected to the Hall of Fame, an honor that was long overdue.

Ron Santo

Santo is easily the best Cubs third baseman of all time. Not only was he a great fielder, but he was one of the most feared sluggers in the National League. He broke in as a 20-year-old rookie in 1960 and retired as a member of the White Sox in 1974.

His achievements are lengthy. Santo led the league seven consecutive years in assists, seven years in putouts, and in double plays six years, at third base. He also smashed 342 home runs among 2,254 career hits. His lifetime batting average is .277.

After leaving baseball, he went into business and later became a member of the Cubs radio broadcast team.

Trivia Questions

1. Where was Santo born?

2. How many home runs did he have in 1961?

3. How many RBIs did he have in 1963?

4. In what year did Santo win his first gold glove?

5. In what year was Santo named Cub captain?

6. What teammate did Santo criticize in 1969 following a tough loss to the Mets?

7. How many RBIs did he have in 1969?

8. When did he collect his 2,000th hit?

9. When did Santo hit his 300th home run?

10. He had a long hitting streak in 1966. How many games did Santo hit in consecutively?

Billy Williams

Williams had one of the "sweetest" swings of all time, which led to a great career and induction into the Hall of Fame in 1987.

Billy grew up in Whistler, Alabama, the youngest of five children. He was signed by the Cubs in 1956, and he played briefly for the big club in 1959 and 1960 before breaking in as a regular in 1961. That season Billy hit .278 with 25 homers and drove in 86 runs. With those totals, he was named the Rookie-of-the-Year.

Chicago Cubs Facts & Trivia

Billy continued to improve as a hitter, and in 1964, he had his first .300 season. He also hit his 100th home run that year. Billy had his greatest season to date in 1965, hitting 34 home runs, driving in 108 runs, and batting .315. His greatest campaign, though, came in 1970 when Billy hit 42 homers, drove in 129 runs, and hit a career high .322. The following season Williams won the batting title.

In 1973, Billy began to slip, and a year later he was traded to the Oakland A's. After two sub-par seasons, he was released.

Trivia Questions

1. What famous Hall-of-Famer helped develolp Williams as a hitter?

2. Billy drove in a run in his first Major League at bat with a ground ball off Jim Owens of the Phillies. Who did Williams drive in?

3. Who did Williams beat out as the 1961 Rookie-of-the-Year?

4. Billy hit a home run in the 1964 All-Star Game. Who did he hit it off?

5. How many consecutive games did he play?

6. When did his consecutive games streak come to an end?

7. Who took Billy's place in left field?

8. As far as salaries go, Williams became the first player for the Cubs to do what?

9. How many career home runs did he have?

10. What was his career batting average?

Don Kessinger

Kessinger is one of the greatest Cub shortstops of all time. His career, though, began slowly. He came up near the end of the 1964 season, but the next spring found himself back in the minors. Then Chicago's regular shortstop, Roberto Pena, made 17 errors in his first 51 games, and Kessinger got another chance. He also was shaky, committing 11 errors in his first nine games. For the season, Kessinger hit just .201 and made 28 errors.

The following year batting coach Pete Reiser taught him to be a switch hitter, and Kessinger hit .274. His fielding also improved and the Cubs boasted perhaps the best infield in all of baseball, with Santo at third, Kessinger at short, Glenn Beckert at second and Ernie Banks at first. The whole infield was selected to the All-Star Game in 1969. Also that year, Kessinger went 54 games without making an error. He also led the team in doubles and runs scored and led National League shortstops in every defensive category. In 1970, he won his second straight Gold Glove Award. In 1972, Don was selected to his fifth straight All-Star Game. In 1975, he passed the legendary Joe Tinker's Cub record for most games played at shortstop. On December 28 of that year, Kessinger was traded to the Cardinals. He moved over to the White Sox where he ended his playing career. He managed the Sox in 1979, but resigned before the end of the season.

Trivia Questions

1. Where was Kessinger born?

2. Where did he go to college?

3. How many triples did he hit in 1970?

4. When did Kessinger appear in his 1,000th Major League game?

5. When did he collect his 1,000th career hit?

6. Who was he traded to the Cardinals for?

7. What was his record as manager of the White Sox?

8. How many games at shortstop did he play for the Cubs?

9. How many career home runs did he have?

10. What was his career batting average?

Glenn Beckert

Beckert started out his professional career as a shortstop, but he learned to play second base after Ken Hubbs was killed. He learned quickly, and in 1965, he was the Cubs starting second baseman. He started out slowly as a hitter but then choked up and started punching the ball and improved his average.

At second base, Beckert teamed with shortstop Don Kessinger to form one of the best double play combinations of all time. Both Beckert and Kessinger played in their 1,000th game on the same day, August 21, 1971.

Beckert continued to improve as a hitter, and in 1971, he hit .342. He also was named to the All-Star Game four years in a row and started in 1968.

On November 12, 1973, Glenn was traded to the Padres. He retired as a Pirate in 1975.

Trivia Questions

1. What was Beckert's nickname?

2. What college did he graduate from?

3. The Cubs claimed Beckert in the December 1962 draft for how much?

4. In 656 at bats in 1965, how many times did Beckert strike out?

5. His longest hitting streak came in 1968. How many straight games did he hit in?

6. In what season did Beckert win the Gold Glove Award?

7. Who did the Cubs trade Beckert to the Padres for?

8. What was Beckert's career batting average?

9. How many hits did he have?

10. How many times did he strike out?

Ferguson Jenkins

Fergie has his place in Cub history for all time. He was one of the team's most dominant pitchers of any era.

The 6'5" right-hander broke into the Majors with the Phillies in late 1965, winning two of three decisions. On April 21, 1966, the Cubs traded two pitchers, Bob Buhl and Larry Jackson, for Jenkins, first baseman John Herrnstein, and outfielder Adolfo Phillips.

In his debut with Chicago, he shut out the Dodgers for six

innings and also hammered a home run. Even at that point, Jenkins thought he belonged in the bullpen. However, later that year, Jenkins moved into the starting rotation and finished the season with a 6-8 record.

From then on, you couldn't get him out of the rotation. When it was Jenkin's turn to pitch, he did. The following year he had his first 20-win season, going 20-13 and leading the league with 20 complete games. His 236 strikeouts set a 20th Century record for a Cub pitcher. He had six consecutive 20-victory seasons before sliding to a 14-16 mark in 1973. During that streak, Fergie had some phenomenal numbers. In 1968, he pitched 308 innings, the first time a Cub pitcher had done that since Charlie Root in 1927. In 1969, he struck out 273 batters, and the following year he whiffed 274.

In 1971, Jenkins won 24 games and appeared in his second All-Star Game. He also led the league in complete games that year with 30. Also that season, Fergie pitched two two-hitters, two three-hitters, and two four-hitters. Always known as a good hitter, he belted six homers in 1971 and drove in 20 runs. Jenkins was the first Cub pitcher to win the Cy Young Award that year.

But after that off year in 1973, he was traded to the Texas Rangers. Fergie bounced back in 1974, going 25-12, the best mark of his career. A year later he was traded to Boston where he spent two seasons before being traded back to the Rangers. After a couple of seasons with the Rangers, Fergie found himself back with the Cubs. He was nearing the end of his career, but he still achieved several milestones before being released in the spring of 1984.

Jenkins was elected to the Hall of Fame in 1991.

Trivia Questions

1. Where was Jenkins born?

2. What was his earned run average in 1968?

3. What was his record in 1969?

4. How many consecutive complete games did he pitch in 1972?

5. When did he strike out his 3,000th batter?

6. What team did it come against?

7. How many career wins did he have?

8. How many games did he lose?

9. What was his lifetime ERA?

10. How many strikeouts did he have?

More Questions About That Era

1. In what year was pitcher Ken Holtzman drafted?

2. His first start came against the Dodgers on April 24, 1966. Who was the opposing pitcher?

3. How did Holtzman do?

4. What was his record in 1967?

5. What did Holtzman do on August 20, 1969?

6. Who was he pitching against?

7. What happened June 3, 1971, at Riverfront Stadium in Cincinnati?

Chicago Cubs Facts & Trivia

8. What was Holtzman's record as a Cub?

9. What was pitcher Bill Hands's record in 1969?

10. What was his ERA that season?

11. What has Hands's record against Cincinnati in 1970?

12. What was his record as a Cub?

13. Catcher Randy Hundley was originally signed by what Major League team?

14. Hundley and Bill Hands were traded to the Cubs on December 2, 1965, for what two players?

15. How many homers did Hundley hit in 1966?

16. How many games did he catch that year?

17. How many games did Hundley catch in 1968?

18. How many homers did he hit as a Cub?

19. What position did Adolfo Phillips play?

20. How many home runs did Jim Hickman hit in August of 1969?

21. What was his average in 1970?

22. How many home runs did he have?

23. How many runs did he drive in that season?

24. How many home runs did Hickman hit as a Cub?

25. What pitch is Phil Regan famous for allegedly throwing?

26. How many pinch-hit homers did Willie Smith hit for the Cubs?

27. How many home runs did Don Young hit in 1969?

28. What did Milt Pappas do on September 2, 1972?

29. What did he almost do in that game?

30 What was Joe Pepitone's average in 1971?

31. What bar did he open in Chicago?

13
TOUGH TIMES

The 1973 Cubs started out playing good baseball and were 46-31 when July rolled around. However, from that point on, they collapsed.

The next season many of the veterans were gone or nearing the end of their careers. Some new additions who played well were center-fielder Rick Monday and right-fielder Jose Cardenal. However, they couldn't prevent the Cubs from finishing last in the National League East.

The following season Chicago finished 5th after a "June Swoon". The Cubs had some good young talent by this time. Third baseman Bill Madlock would go on to win a couple of batting titles with the Cubs, and Manny Trillo played a solid second base. Pitching was still a problem, and in 1976, Chicago finished 4th.

After the season, Jim Marshall, who had replaced Whitey Lockman as manager following the 1974 season, was himself replaced by Herman Franks. Bob Kennedy was also named the new general manager. When Madlock and Monday demanded more money, they were traded. The Cubs then picked up Bobby Murcer.

On April 12, 1977, Phil Wrigley died, and ownership of the team passed to his son William.

The Cubs that year finished 4th with an 81-81 record. At one point in the season, Chicago had been 47-22, but then the teams ace relief pitcher Bruce Sutter, with the wicked split-finger fastball, went down for a while, and the Cubs faltered.

Besides Sutter, another bright spot for Chicago that year was shortstop Ivan DeJesus, whom the Cubs picked up in the Rick Monday trade. Also, Bill Buckner arrived from the Dodgers and became one of the team's better hitters.

In 1978, the Cubs finished 3rd even though their record was below .500. Chicago picked up slugger Dave Kingman that season, but as a team only hit 72 home runs. However, the following year "King Kong" belted 48 homers and Sutter had 37 saves, but in the end, the Cubs could only finish in 5th place. With a week left in the season, Herman Franks resigned and was temporarily replaced by Joe Amalfitano.

In 1980, Chicago hired Preston Gomez, a proven loser. He was no inspiration, and the Cubs finished last. Gomez was replaced after 90 games by Amalfitano as Chicago limped through another disappointing season.

SOME PLAYERS OF THAT ERA

Rick Monday

Rick Monday broke in with the then Kansas City A's late in the 1966 season.

After hitting .290 in 1970, Monday's average sank to .245 the following year. Rick was then traded to the Cubs for pitcher Ken Holtzman.

Monday was moved to the leadoff spot, and in 1973, he smashed 26 home runs. He was also good in the field and ran the bases well.

In 1976, his last year with the Cubs, Monday hit 32 home runs. After the season, he was traded to the Dodgers along with relief pitcher Mike Garman for Bill Buckner, Ivan DeJesus, and minor league pitcher Jeff Albert.

Chicago Cubs Facts & Trivia

Trivia Questions

1. What did Monday do on April 25, 1976?

2. Why is that date special in Cubs history?

3. How many hits did Monday have in that game?

4. How many homers did he have in his career?

5. How many homers did he have as a Cub?

Bill Madlock

The Cubs picked up Madlock from the Texas Rangers in a trade after the 1973 season. Besides Madlock, Chicago also received Vic Harris. In return, the Rangers received Ferguson Jenkins.

Madlock was a solid hitter for the Cubs right from the start. In 1974, he hit .313 to lead the team. He followed that up with a league-leading .354 mark in 1975, then beat out Ken Griffey, Sr., on the last day of the 1976 season to win the batting crown for the second consecutive year, this time with a .339 average.

After that season, Madlock wanted a five-year contract for around a million dollars, but the Cubs refused. He was dealt to the Giants, then went to the Pirate where he won two more batting titles and helped Pittsburgh win the 1979 World Series. But once again, the Cubs let a star player go to save money.

Trivia Questions

1. What team first signed Madlock?

2. Who did he replace at third base for the Cubs?

3. What was Madlock's three-year batting average with the Cubs?

4. In the 1975 All-Star Game, he earned co-MVP honors with whom?

5. Madlock and Rob Sperring were traded by the Cubs to the Giants. Name the players the Cubs got in return.

Rick Reuschel

Reuschel was one of the few bright spots on the Cubs pitching staff through the '70s. He broke in with Chicago in 1972 and finished his rookie season with a 10-8 record. With a very poor club the following season, Rick was 14-15.

The following season his brother Paul also joined the Cubs. Paul was a reliever in parts of four seasons with Chicago, while Rick continued to start and remain the club's ace. In 1977, he won 20 games while losing 10.

Then on June 12, 1981, Reuschel was traded to the Yanks in a multi-player deal. The Cubs also received $400,000.

A couple of years later Rick was back with the Cubs, but he wasn't the Reuschel of old. Although at 35, he wasn't washed up. In fact, he had successful seasons with the Pirates and the Giants before retiring in the early 1990s with over 200 wins.

As a Cub he won 135 and lost 127. He was a battler and a true Cub all the way!

Trivia Questions

1. Where was Reuschel born?

2. In what year was he signed by the Cubs?

Chicago Cubs Facts & Trivia

3. Against what team did Rick win his first Major League game?

4. What did Reuschel do in his first Major League at bat?

5. How many batters did he strike out as a Cub pitcher?

Other Questions About That Era

1. What kind of pitch was Burt Hooton known for?

2. He pitched a no-hitter on April 15, 1972 against what team?

3. What was the score?

4. How many batters did he walk?

5. What team did the Cubs trade Hooton to?

6. Who did the Cubs trade to the Milwaukee Brewers for Jose Cardenal?

7. In what year did Jose have his first .300 season?

8. Cardenal had his best season in 1975. What was his average?

9. How many stolen bases did he have that year?

10. How many lifetime hits did he have?

11. What was Ray Burris's record in 1975?

12. What was Whitey Lockman's record as Cubs manager?

13. How many RBIs did Jerry Morales have in 1974?

14. In 1975, he led the club in RBIs. How many did he have?

15. How many home runs did he hit that year?

16. How many years did Manny Trillo play with the Cubs?

17. What was pitcher Steve Stone's three-year record with the Cubs?

18. On April 17, 1974, George Mitterwald hit three home runs in a game. Against what team did he accomplish the feat?

19. Catcher Steve Swisher was selected to the National League All-Star team in what year?

20. This player hit three home runs in one game in his Cub debut. Who was he?

21. What was Larry Biittner's average for the Cubs in 1977?

22. What was his lifetime average?

23. In what year was Bruce Sutter signed to a Cub contract?

24. What pitch was Sutter known for?

25. In what year was Sutter the Rookie-of-the-Year.

26. What was his ERA that year?

27. How many saves did Sutter have in 1977?

Chicago Cubs Facts & Trivia

28. What was his ERA that year?

29. Sutter won two All-Star Games. In what year did he win his first?

30. In what year did he win the Cy Young Award?

31. How many saves did he have that season?

32. What team was Sutter traded to?

33. What was Herman Franks's three-year record as Cub manager?

34. In 7½ season with the Cubs, what was Bill Buckner's batting average?

35. What was Buckner's average in 1978?

36. In 1980, he won the league batting title. What was his average?

37. In 614 trips to the plate, how many times did he strike out?

38. How many hits did Buckner have in 1982?

39. How many runs did he drive in that season?

40. What team did the Cubs trade Buckner to?

41. What position did Ivan De Jesus play?

42. How many stolen bases did he have in 1980?

43. Ivan was traded to the Phillies for what two players?

44. How many home runs did Bobby Murcer hit in 1977, his first year with the Cubs?

45. How long did he play for the Cubs?

46. What was the managerial record of Preston Gomez when he managed the Cubs?

47. In Dave Kingman's first year with the Cubs, how many home runs did he hit?

48. How many homers did Kingman hit in 1979?

49. How many runs did he drive in that year?

50. Kingman was traded to what team?

14
CLOSE BUT NO CIGAR: FUTILITY LIVES!

The turnaround for the Cubs in the 1980s occurred when Dallas Green, who had been the general manager for the Phillies, was hired in the same capacity for the Cubs. It was in October 1981 when Green came to Chicago. Earlier that summer, on June 12, Major League players walked away from their jobs because of the free agency issue. Just a few days later, on June 16, William Wrigley announced the Cubs had been sold to the Chicago Tribune Company.

After a last place finish in 1981, the Cubs rose a notch to 5th place in 1982. Young players like Ryne Sandberg, Leon Durham, and Jody Davis showed promise; veteran pitcher Fergie Jenkins had a pretty good year; and the bullpen, consisting of Lee Smith, Bill Campbell, and Mike Proly, performed well. The club seemed to respond to new manager Lee Elia.

But in 1983, the club faltered, and Elia was replaced by Administrative Assistant Charlie Fox, who took over as interim manager. However, nothing could help the Cubs, who finished 5th again.

After the season, Jim Frey, who had led the Royals to a pennant in 1980, was named the new manager.

The Cubs started out spring training in 1984 on a lousy note with a 7-20 record. Then just before the season began Green made a solid trade with the Phillies. He sent relief pitcher Bill Campbell and rookie catcher Mike Diaz to Philadelphia for outfielders Gary Matthews and Bob Dernier, and pitcher Porfirio Altamirano. With Dernier leading off, Matthews batting third, and Ryne Sandberg sandwiched between them in the lineup, Chicago started winning.

Green wasn't done dealing. On May 25, he sent first sacker Bill Buckner and minor league infielder Mike Brumley to Boston for starting pitcher Dennis Eckersley. A little more than two weeks later he sent promising outfielders Mel Hall and Joe Carter and a minor league pitcher to Cleveland for starting pitcher Rick Sutcliffe. The Cubs now had a sound rotation of Sutcliffe, Eckersley, Dick Ruthven (acquired the year before by Green from Philadelphia), Steve Trout (acquired by Green from the White Sox a year earlier), and Scott Sanderson (acquired from San Diego the winter before). Tim Stoddard acted as the setup man for ace stopper Lee Smith in the bullpen.

The Cubs didn't swoon that year and won the East Division Championship on September 24 as Rick Sutcliffe beat the Pirates, 4-1. But after winning the first two playoff games from the San Diego Padres, Chicago lost the next three games, and Cub fans had to watch the World Series on television.

After the exciting 1984 season, fans expected more of the same the following year. Through the middle of June, the Cubs appeared to be on their way to another division crown with a 5½-games lead over the Mets. Then fleet-footed centerfielder Bob Dernier went on the disabled list, and in turn, each of the starting pitchers joined him there until at one point all five starters were on the DL together. The Cubs stumbled in with a 77-84 record and a 4th place finish in the division.

After a poor start in 1986, Frey's days as manager of the Cubs were numbered. After 56 games, he was replaced by Gene Michael who could do little better. Then Michael quit with a month to go in 1987 and his team at the .500 mark. His replacement was Frank Lucchesi, another proven loser, and the Cubs finished 6th, a notch below the previous year.

After a year in the broadcast booth, Jim Frey replaced

Dallas Green in the front office, and he hired old pal Don Zimmer to be field boss in 1988. The Cubs won just one more game than the previous year, but they climbed to 4th in the division.

Not much was expected when 1989 rolled around, but then everything seemed to come together for the Cubs. With Zimmer managing by the seat of his pants, the Cubs finished at 93-69 and on top of the NL East. Zimmer was named the National League Manager-of-the-Year. Center fielder Jerome Walton had a great first year and was named the Rookie-of-the-Year. However, the Cubs were once again unable to get to the World Series. This time the Giants took Chicago in five games.

From 1990-1993, the Cubs finished in 4th place each year. After a disappointing 77-85 season in 1990, especially after the success of the previous year, Zimmer was replaced a quarter of the way through 1991 by Jim Essian, who finished at 59-63.

Frey was subsequently replaced in the front office by Larry Himes, and he hired Jim Lefebvre as manager. Under Lefebvre, the Cubs finished at 78-84 in 1992 and 84-78 in 1993. Himes and Lefebvre had a falling out, and coach Tom Trebelhorn, the former manager of the Milwaukee Brewers, was hired for the strike-shortend year of 1994. He was not an improvement as he led the Cubs to a 49-64 mark.

When 1995 rolled around, Trebelhorn was gone and so was Himes. Sound baseball man Andy McPhail had been named president and CEO of the Cubs, and he hired Ed Lynch to be general manager. Lynch, in turn, hired former San Diego manager Jim Riggleman to be the new manager. In another strike-shortened season, he led the Cubs to a 73-71 record, which was good for third place in the National League Central Division, but still 12 games behind division winner Cincinnati.

Now, it's time for another season to roll around. Will the 1996 Cubs be any better than last year or any of the previous years? That remains to be seen.

But one thing is for sure, and that is, the Cubs will always provide excitement. They may make you happy or they may break your heart. But, if you're a Cubs fan, it doesn't really make any difference because you know the CUBS ARE TRADITION and you'll both be back next year!

SOME STARS OF THAT ERA

Keith Moreland

From 1982 thru' 87, Moreland was one of the players that held the Cubs together. Although not a superstar, he was always dangerous in the clutch and was one of the main contributors in the 1984 Division Championship season. He had 11 game-winning hits, 3rd best on the team, and stroked 16 homers and drove in 80 runs, while batting .279 that season.

The following year he hit .307 and drove in 106 runs to lead the Cubs in both categories. His highest home run total came in 1989, when he hit 27.

Although never a great fielder, he caught for the Cubs, played right field, then was switched to third base 1987.

In February of 1988, Moreland was traded to San Diego, then he split the 1989 season between Detroit and Baltimore.

Trivia Questions

1. What was Keith's average in 1983?

2. In 1984, he won National League Player-of-the-Month honors for what month?

3. What did Moreland hit in the playoffs that year?

4. In 1985, what was Keith's average with men in scoring position?

5. How many assists did he have as a right-fielder in 1986?

Gary Matthews

The "Sarge" was a true leader and showed that during the 1984 season. He was the holler guy the Cubs lacked.

Before coming to the Cubs in late March of that year, Matthews had played for the Giants, Braves, and Phillies, and had a solid career.

"Sarge" started off quickly in 1984 and hit safely in 13 of his first 15 games, while hustling out in left field. He proved to be a great clutch-hitter, and his 19th game winning RBI that season clinched the National League East Division title for the Cubs.

The following year he had knee surgery at mid-season and played in only 97 games, but he bounced back the next year to tie for the team leadership in home runs with 21.

In mid-1987, Sarge was traded to Seattle.

Trivia Questions

1. What was Matthews's average in 1984?

2. How many runs did he drive in that year?

3. He also led the team in walks with how many?

4. How many runs did he score?

5. How many games did play in 1987?

Rick Sutcliffe

The real key to the Cubs turnaround in 1984 came on June

15 when Sutcliffe was acquired from the Cleveland Indians. He went 16-1 with the Cubs and finished the season at 20-6 overall. Sutcliffe could do no wrong that year and was the winning pitcher on September 24 against the Pirates when Chicago won the East Division crown.

After that great season, injuries set in, and Rick was only 5-3 in 1985. He was pretty healthy in 1986, but not very lucky, as his record was only 5-14. But in those 14 losses, the Cubs only scored 23 runs for him!

Rick bounced back the next year to win 18 games and just missed the Cy Young Award. In 1988, he dipped to 13-14, but once again received no support. When the Cubs won the East Division crown again in 1989, he responded with a 16-11 record, with many of those wins coming in the clutch. Injuries took their toll again in 1990, and he was 0-2 before closing out his Cub career with a 6-5 mark in 1991.

Trivia Questions

1. Sutcliffe was originally drafted by what team?

2. In 1979, he was the Rookie-of-the-Year. What was his record?

3. Name the Cub players that went to Cleveland in the trade for Sutcliffe?

4. When did he strike out his 1,000th batter?

5. What was his won-loss record as a Cub?

Andre Dawson

Dawson played with the Cubs from 1987 thru '92 and put up some big numbers. He socked 49 homers and drove in 137 runs in '87 after being signed as a free agent that spring.

The next year his homer and RBI totals dipped, but he still led the Cubs with 24 dingers and 79 RBIs while hitting .303. He also continued to be good defensively in right field, and he possessed one of the strongest arms in baseball.

Dawson missed a portion of the 1989 season, but he still hit 21 homers to help the Cubs win the East title. In 1990, at the age of 35, Andre belted 27 homers, drove in 100 runs, and batted .310. He had another very productive season the following year.

Since leaving the Cubs, Andre has played for Boston and last season with the Florida Marlins and at the age of 4l, still feels he has some baseball left in him.

Trivia Questions

1. What is Andre's nickname?

2. What Major League team did he break in with?

3. How many home runs did he hit in 1991?

4. How many runs did he drive in that season?

5. In what year did Dawson in the National League MVP Award?

Mark Grace

Since breaking in with Chicago in 1988, Grace has compiled a .306 lifetime average. That includes a .325 mark in 1993, which was the highest mark for a Cub since Bill Madlock hit .339 in 1976. He also had 14 homers and drove in 98 runs that season. In 1995, he had his highest average to date, hitting .326. He also led the league with 51 doubles and hammered 16 homers, while driving in 92 runs.

Grace is also one of the best first baseman in the Majors and has won several Gold Glove Awards, beginning in 1992. He also is looked to as a leader and would be sorely missed if he should ever leave the team. Although he'll be 32 in June 1996, he is still in the prime of his career and should have lots of productive seasons left.

Trivia Questions

1. Grace was the first rookie to lead the team in walks since who?

2. What was his batting average in 1989?

3. How many hits did he have in 1993?

4. How many times did Grace strike out in 1995?

5. What two colleges did he attend?

Ryne Sandberg

HE'S BACK!!!!!

Cubs fans have to be very happy that, arguably, the best second baseman to ever play the game will be back in a Chicago Cubs uniform for the 1996 season.

After stunning Cubs fans in the summer of '94 with the announcement of his retirement, Ryno surprised and delighted an equal number of fans when he announced his return to the Cubs in the fall of 1995. Quitting after 13 seasons, Ryno said the game was no longer fun and he didn't compete on the high level he had been used to. However, a new marriage and a rekindled love for baseball, prompted his return. Sandberg said he wants again to compete and feels he has something to offer.

Chicago Cubs Facts & Trivia

He has been to the All-Star Game 10 times and has won nine Gold Glove Awards.

Ryno broke in with the Phillies in 1981, playing 13 games. The next season he found himself in a Cubs uniform and started the campagin at third base. Later that year, he was moved to second base, and his legend began.

In 1983, he won his first Gold Glove Award, and in so doing, he became the first player in league history to win a Gold Glove in his first full season at a new position.

Perhaps his greatest season came in 1984 when he was named the National League MVP. He hit .314 that season, with 200 hits, 36 doubles, 19 triples, and 19 home runs. He also drove in 84 and scored 114, tops in the league. He tied for the league lead in triples. In addition, he swiped 32 bases, and his fielding, of course, was flawless.

Another great statistical season came in 1990 when he smashed 40 home runs, becoming just the third second baseman in Major League history to hit 40 homers in a season. He also became the first player in the history of the game to have a 40-homer season and also have a season in which he stole 50 or more bases, having 54 thefts in 1985.

Going into the '96 season, in his second stint with the Cubs, Ryne has hit 240 home runs as a second baseman. That's 4th on the all time list. He also ranks in the Cubs top 10 in 10 major offensive categories. And the good thing about all that is, there's more to come.

The 35-year-old Sandberg is a sure bet for the Hall of Fame, but there's still some goals he'd like to accomplish. The foremost is contributing to a team that makes it back to the playoffs and advances on to the World Series, something the Cubs haven't done since 1945. Now, wouldn't that be great!

WELCOME BACK, RYNO!

Trivia Questions

1. What was Sandberg's batting average in 1982?

2. How many times has he hit over 30 home runs in a season?

3. How many career home runs does he have?

4. How many lifetime hits does he have?

5. What's his lifetime batting average?

6. How many times has he scored over 100 runs in a season?

7. How many times has he drove in 100 runs in a season?

8. How many years has he hit .300?

9. Going into the '96 season, his fielding average is the highest in Major League history. What is it?

10. How many times has he had 200 hits in a season?

11. When will he be elected to the Hall of Fame?

More Questions About That Era

1. What team did Dallas Green manage to a World Series win before taking over as Cubs general manager?

2. In what year did he resign?

3. What was Don Zimmer's record as manager of the Cubs?

4. How long did Larry Bowa play with the Cubs?

5. How many home runs did Leon Durham hit in 1984?

Chicago Cubs Facts & Trivia

6. How many runs did he drive in?

7. How many years did Leon play for the Cubs?

8. How many RBIs did Jody Davis have in 1984?

9. How many home runs did he hit it 1983?

10. How long did Lee Smith play for Chicago?

11. How many saves did Smith have in 1983?

12. What was Lee Elia's record as Cubs manager?

13. How many RBIs did Ron Cey have in 1983?

14. How many in 1984?

15. How many home runs did he have in 1984?

16. What is his nickname?

17. What team did the Cubs trade Cey to on January 30, 1987?

18. Davey Lopes hit his 100th home run in a Cub uniform. When did he accomplish that milestone?

19. What was pitcher Steve Trout's nickname?

20. What was Bob Dernier's average in 1984?

21. What position did he play?

22. How many games did Dennis Eckersley win as a Cub?

23. How many did he lose?

24. When did Shawon Dunston break into the majors with the Cubs?

25. How many home runs does he have going into the '96 season?

26. What was his 1995 batting average?

27. What pick was Dunston overall in the 1982 draft?

28. Who was the Cubs first pick in the 1985 draft?

29. When did the Cubs play their first night game in Wrigley Field?

30. That first game was rained out in the 4th inning. The next night the first "official" night game was completed at Wrigley Field. Who did the Cubs beat?

31. What was Vance Law's batting average in 1988?

32. How many years did Jerome Walton play with the Cubs?

33. 1996 will mark how many years that Harry Caray has broadcast Major League Baseball?

34. What was Jaime Navarro's record for the Cubs in 1995?

35. How long did Greg Maddox pitch for the Cubs?

36. How many home runs did Sammy Sosa hit in 1995?

37. How many runs did he drive in?

Chicago Cubs Facts & Trivia

38. What Major League team did Sosa break in with?

39. How many career home runs does he have?

40. What did Brian McRae hit for the Cubs in 1995?

41. How many saves did Randy Myers have for the Cubs in 1995?

42. Myers led the National League with how many saves in 1993?

43. How many career home runs going into the '96 season, does Ray Sanchez have?

44. How many years did Rick Wilkins play with the Cubs?

45. What was his batting average in 1993?

46. Who is the Cubs current general manager?

47. Going into the 1996 season, what is the Cubs record against the rest of the National League?

48. What team do the Cubs have the most lifetime wins against?

49. This broadcaster will join Ron Santo in the broadcast booth and do the radio play-by-play for the '96 season. He's a former Brewers announcer. Who is he?

50. When will the Cubs win the World Series?

THE ANSWERS

1 - EARLY CUBS

1. April 25
2. Chicago
3. Louisville
4. 4-0
5. Eight
6. Burlington Flats, New York
7. 1832
8. 49
9. Byron
10. Rockford
11. Forest City Team
12. 15
13. Boston Red Stockings
14. 207
15. 57
16. 1875
17. 46
18. 12
19. 529
20. 8
21. 45 feet
22. First Base
23. 1878
24. 1882
25. *The Sporting News*
26. Bob Ferguson
27. Hot Springs, Arkansas
28. 1886
29. James Hart
30. James 'Deacon' White
31. That baseball had been invented in Cooperstown.
32. 1946
33. May 10
34. 23rd and State streets
35. 6-0, Chicago
36. Second base
37. Hit the first home run in National League history
38. .404
39. None
40. Shortstop
41. 'Death to Flying Things'
42. Left field
43. Come to bat 500 times in a season
44. .288
45. Frank 'Terry' Larkin
46. 89-80
47. Hit in the head by a line drive
48. Catcher
49. 'Old Silver'
50. A glove

2 - ADRIAN 'CAP' ANSON: THE FIRST STAR

1. Marshalltown, Iowa
2. April 17, 1852
3. Notre Dame
4. One year
5. Rockford
6. .421
7. 1887
8. Five
9. .333
10. Hit a home run
11. July 18, 1897
12. 3,041
13. 97
14. 1,719
15. 1,879
16. 1,288
17. 944
18. .302
19. 9th place
20. April 14, 1922

3 - OTHER EARLY STARS

Ed Williamson
1. Philadelphia
2. Babe Ruth

3. Ned
4. Indianapolis
5. 1878
6. Seven times
7. Four times
8. 1886
9. 1,159
10. .255

King Kelly
1. Cincinnati Reds
2. Two
3. .354 in 1884 and .388 in 1886
4. Three
5. Three
6. *Slide, Kelly, Slide*
7. Signaling pitches
8. Boston of The Players League
9. 1,820
10. .307

Bill Hutchison
1. December 17, 1859
2. New Haven, Connecticut
3. Yale University
4. He did not play minor league baseball
5. 16-17
6. Twice
7. 43
8. 'Wild Bill'
9. Won both ends of a doubleheader
10. 183-160, 3.60 ERA

Clark Griffith
1. November 20, 1868
2. Stringtown, Missouri
3. 2-0
4. Cincinnati Reds
5. 14 innings
6. Rube Waddel

7. Pittsburgh Pirates
8. Griffith
9. 242-131
10. 3.31

Jimmy Ryan
1. 356
2. .306
3. .360
4. 16
5. Six
6. 1,093
7. Eight times
8. 140
9. 1889
10. 4-0
11. Three
12. 2,531
13. 2,102
14. 1,640
15. .310

Fred Pfeffer
1. Louisville, Kentucky
2. 'Unser Fritz'
3. 400 feet
4. .289
5. 1884
6. Louisville Colonels
7. 16
8. .255
9. 1,671
10. 1,670
11. University of Wisconsin

Tommy Burns
1. Hornell
2. Three
3. Three
4. Three
5. Two doubles and a home run
6. Four
7. 86

8. .264
9. 1,299
10. 160-138

More Trivia Questions About That Era

1. Fred Goldsmith
2. 18
3. Brooklyn, New York
4. August 16, 1870
5. 43
6. 14
7. A submarine ball
8. 268
9. 60
10. 57
11. Boston
12. 137
13. 57
14. Providence Grays
15. Won his 50th game
16. 53
17. 16
18. 623
19. 318
20. 68
21. 10
22. 36
23. 340
24. 38
25. Boston
26. $10,000
27. 1963
28. Jim McCormick
29. 16
30. George Van Haltron
31. Boston
32. Pittsburgh Pirates
33. June 21, 1888
34. .309
35. 1888
36. .305
37. 12
38. Bill Dahlen
39. 1894
40. 'Bad'
41. Five seasons
42. .291
43. Boston Spiders
44. Jim Whitney
45. Pittsburgh
46. Phillies
47. 39 years
48. Three times
49. 14
50. Center field
51. Walked six times
52. Cleveland
53. .330
54. 134 runs
55. 130
56. 197
57. New York
58. .276
59. Six seasons
60. .313
61. 92
62. Hit a 500-foot home run
63. Seven years
64. 84
65. 73
66. .389
67. 120
68. 10
69. .330
70. 1,055
71. 399
72. 28
73. San Francisco
74. Billy Schriver
75. One
76. .264
77. .358
78. 1895
79. 197
80. Walt Wilmot
81. 75 errors

82. First base
83. 902
84. .317
85. 36
86. Louisville
87. 'Barry'
88. Walt Thornton
89. The Cardinals
90. 'Danny'
91. .293
92. 1,021
93. First base
94. 1898
95. Hit leadoff home runs
96. The Cardinals
97. 10
98. .279
99. Herbert Briggs
100. 'Buttons'

4 - THE EARLY YEARS OF THE 20TH CENTURY

SOME STARS OF THAT ERA

Frank Chance
1. 67
2. Hit for the cycle
3. Five
4. .327
5. .421
6. 530
7. .693
8. .297
9. 1,276
10. 405
11. 1946
12. Joe Tinker and Johnny Evers

Johnny Kling
1. Four times
2. Six

3. Two
4. Once
5. Jimmy Archer
6. September 11, 1900
7. New York Giants
8. Three
9. .271
10. 1,151
11. 123

Johnny Evers
1. July 21, 1881
2. Troy, New York
3. 'Trojan' and 'Crab'
4. 49
5. 46
6. .300
7. .270
8. 1,658
9. 324
10. St. Mary's Cemetery in Troy, New York

Joe Tinker
1. July 27, 1880
2. Muscotah, Kansas
3. 5'9" and 175 pounds
4. Hit a World Series home run
5. 41
6. He stole home twice in one game
7. Five times
8. Four times
9. Twice
10. Once
11. .263

Mordecai Brown
1. Third baseman
2. 29
3. 1908
4. 11
5. Nine

6. 58
7. 24
8. 13
9. Nine
10. 239-130
11. Five
12. Terre Haute, Indiana
13. 1949
14. Five

Frank Schulte
1. 'Wildfire'
2. .389
3. Ring Lardner
4. 10
5. 21
6. 107
7. 105
8. 30
9. 21
10. .300 and .534
11. 23
12. Hit 20 or more doubles, triples, homers and stolen bases
13. Four
14. 44 years
15. 1,766
16. .270

Heinie Zimmerman
1. .372
2. 207
3. 14
4. 99
5. 23 games
6. He drove in nine runs
7. Braves
8. He was ejected from the game
9. 1,566
10. .295

More Trivia Questions About That Era

1. Jack Taylor. He finished all 187 of his starts
2. 'Brakeman Jack'
3. 97 percent
4. Tom Loftus
5. A 5th place tie in 1900 and 6th in 1901
6. Tully Hartsel
7. 'Topsy'
8. .335
9. 187
10. Philadelphia Athletics
11. 14-14
12. 91-54
13. 1902-1909
14. 1.17
15. The first Tinker-to-Evers-to Chance double play occurred
16. 'The Human Icicle'
17. Because he was an effective pitcher in cold weather
18. Coached college baseball
19. Colts
20. 'Shorty' and 'The Rabbit'
21. 27
22. Six
23. 10
24. .268
25. 273
26. Two home runs
27. 97-72
28. The Reds and Giants
29. 'Tornado Jake'
30. 64-53
31. 'Iron Man' Joe McGinnity
32. The Cardinals
33. 20-9
34. Orval Overall
35. Pitcher and Catcher
36. 1904
37. 'Circus Solly'

Chicago Cubs Facts & Trivia

38. .304
39. Center field
40. .285
41. .325
42. 1,094
43. .269
44. 18-13
45. 'Big Ed'
46. 20 innings
47. 19-4
48. 12
49. He pitched a one-hitter
50. 1945
51. 24-7
52. He pitched two shutouts
53. Only once
54. The Dodgers
55. 5-0 and 3-0
56. Four
57. 60 years. It was tied by Cub Mordecai Brown that season, tied again by Cub Bill Lee in 1938, and finally broken by Dodger Don Drysdale with six consecutives shutouts in 1968.
58. 14
59. 185-104
60. Cincinnati Reds
61. 1906
62. University of California
63. 12-3
64. 23-8
65. 1.70
66. Eight
67. 6-1
68. 21
69. 205
70. Ferguson Jenkins in 1967 with 236 strikeouts
71. 108-70
72. 2.24
73. Seven
74. 147
75. 1945
76. Ed Stanky
77. 1906-1912
78. Left field
79. Harry Steinfeldt
80. .327
81. Dublin, Ireland
82. Catcher
83. He developed the snap throw from a squatting position
84. Nine seasons
85. 81
86. Leonard
87. 20
88. He pitched a seven-inning no-hitter
89. It had to be called so both teams could catch a train
90. 55-27
91. Larry Cheney
92. 28
93. 14
94. Wilbur Good
95. Grover Alexander
96. Jimmy Lavender
97. The Spitball
98. Pitcher
99. Shin Guards
100. Washington
101. 1900
102. 1913
103. 4th place
104. 1945
105. Hank O'Day
106. He was an umpire

5 - WRIGLEY TAKES OVER

SOME PLAYERS OF THE TEENS AND '20S

Grover Alexander
1. 51
2. 58 minutes
3. The Braves
4. 3-0
5. 363
6. 1.91
7. 173
8. September 20, 1924
9. The Giants
10. 7-3 (12 innings)
11. 19 innings
12. Cleveland

Bill Killefer
1. Bloomington, Michigan
2. October 10, 1887
3. 'Reindeer Bill'
4. The Browns
5. 1909
6. 1911
7. $60,000
8. .118
9. 299-292
10. 72

Hack Miller
1. Lawrence
2. From a wrestler named Hackenschmidt
3. 164
4. From 47-67 ounces
5. .429
6. A rolled up baseball cap
7. 5'9" - 208 pounds
8. .279
9. Oakland, California
10. September 17, 1971

Hippo Vaughn
1. James
2. Each threw nine hitless innings
3. The Reds in 10 innings
4. 1-0
5. 22
6. 148
7. Eight
8. 1.74
9. 290
10. 33
11. Two
12. Became the last Cub pitcher to steal home
13. 3-0
14. 178-137
15. 2.49

Fred Mitchell
1. Yapp
2. It was his mothers maiden name
3. Because he thought Yapp would make him the butt of jokes
4. Four years
5. One
6. Fifth, first, third and fifth
7. 308-269
8. 194-131 and five ties
9. 30-48
10. 92

More Trivia Questions About This Era

1. Frank Chance
2. 1911
3. 14
4. 21
5. 18
6. Christy Mathewson
7. Five

Chicago Cubs Facts & Trivia

8. .263
9. He broke his leg
10. 1919
11. The Pirates
12. None
13. 13
14. 12
15. George Paskert
16. 34
17. Become an architect
18. Center field
19. Catcher
20. 18
21. .324
22. 84
23. Gabby Harnett
24. The Cardinals
25. Babe Ruth
26. 'Shufflin'
27. Max Flack
28. Cliff Heathcote
29. 20-7
30. It was alleged Hendrix sent a wire to a gambler, placing a $5,000 bet against the Cubs
31. 1917
32. Four seasons
33. .314
34. Vic Aldridge
35. All singles
36. Shortstop
37. .316
38. 161
39. .340
40. 201
41. Five, which set a league record
42. 28
43. .304
44. He committed suicide
45. He single-handedly rescued 15 children from a burning building
46. 19-9
47. Eight
48. He pitched a 21-inning complete game
49. 1919
50. .318
51. All nine
52. Tony Kaufmann
53. The Phillies
54. 26-23
55. Zeb Terry
56. .300
57. 1921
58. .321
59. Oscar
60. 'Bummer'
61. He drove in the tying and winning runs on both days
62. 17
63. .354
64. 45
65. .329
66. 5' 5½"
67. 'Sparky'
68. Rabbit Maranville
69. 1925
70. .309
71. He hit two doubles
72. 55
73. 44
74. Second base
75. 'Boots'
76. Two
77. 1926
78. Struck out
79. .319
80. 209
81. One
82. Maranville was named Cubs manager
83. George Gibson
84. Being the only Canadian to manage a big league club
85. Rabbit Maranville
86. 12-14

6 - THE JOE MCCARTHY ERA

SOME STARS OF THE ERA

Joe McCarthy
1. Philadelphia
2. 82-72
3. The Athletics scored 10 runs
4. 10-8
5. 442-321
6. New York Yankees
7. Eight
8. Seven
9. Boston Red Sox
10. 1957

Rogers Hornsby
1. Winters, Texas
2. .402
3. New York Giants
4. 229
5. 156
6. He hit three straight home runs
7. Eight runs
8. Charlie Grimm
9. .358
10. 1942

Hack Wilson
1. $7,500
2. 190
3. 244
4. 39
5. 159
6. Mule Haas
7. Art Shires
8. None
9. 1,461
10. .307

More Questions About This Era

1. The Browns
2. 0-4
3. 201
4. 201-160
5. 26
6. 'Strongheart'
7. 5th inning
8. 42
9. The Boston Braves
10. 6-4
11. 111
12. 49
13. 3-1
14. 1933
15. 152-101
16. He gave up the final two home runs of Babe Ruth's career. Nos. 713 and 714
17. .336
18. .367
19. Left field
20. Two
21. Old Hoss
22. Jimmy Cooney, Jr.
23. Shortstop
24. Pittsburgh's Paul Waner
25. Hal Carlson
26. .335
27. 214
28. 152
29. 400
30. Rogers Hornsby
31. Pat Malone
32. 115-79
33. Hazen
34. Pirates
35. Stolen bases
36. .360
37. 102
38. 228
39. 50

Chicago Cubs Facts & Trivia

40. .321
41. 2,229
42. 127
43. 328
44. 50
45. 1968

7 - REBUILDING AND SUCCESS

SOME STARS OF THAT ERA

Gabby Hartnett
1. A triple
2. 37
3. 122
4. 1935
5. .344
6. .354
7. Kansas City A's
8. .297
9. 12 years
10. 231

Charlie Grimm
1. .091
2. .995
3. .345
4. 194
5. .389
6. Phil Cavarretta
7. Nine times
8. 2,299
9. 1,708
10. .290

Billy Herman
1. William Jennings Bryan Herman
2. 206
3. Five seasons
4. 'Owl Eyes' and 'Old Popeyes'

5. 57 doubles each year
6. 227
7. .341
8. Four
9. 2,345
10. .304

More Questions About That Era

1. Johnny Moore
2. 13
3. 'Arkansas Hummingbird'
4. 22
5. 2.37
6. Two
7. He became an umpire
8. .272
9. Kiki Cuyler
10. 212
11. Billy Jurges
12. Boston Red Sox
13. Two years
14. 20
15. Philadelphia Phillies
16. $40,000
17. He threw successive shutouts
18. 13-14
19. 20-6
20. Five
21. 22-9
22. 2.66
23. Nine
24. 139-123
25. Hitting into a double play
26. Homered from both sides of the plate in one game
27. 203
28. "Goo-Goo"
29. 95
30. 21
31. James
32. First base

33. He played the entire game at first base with no putouts or assists
34. $185,000
35. 7-1
36. 16-8
37. 1939
38. Center field
39. .288
40. Three
41. One season
42. 34

8 - THE WAR-TIME CUBS

SOME PLAYERS OF THAT ERA

Stan Hack
1. Sacramento of the Pacific Coast League
2. 'Smiling Stan'
3. Scoring 100 or more runs for six straight years
4. August 30, 1945
5. A single
6. Preacher Roe of the Pirates
7. Eight
8. 6th
9. 2,193
10. .301

Phil Cavarretta
1. Phillibuck
2. 12
3. 154
4. .321
5. 152
6. 82
7. 97
8. #44
9. 1,977
10. .293

Claude Passeau
1. 162-150
2. 124-94
3. He fielded 273 chances without making an error
4. 'Mr. Chips'
5. Oufielder Joe Marty and Pitchers Kirby Higbe and Ray Harrell
6. Millsaps College
7. Bachelor of Science Degree
8. Hit a grand slam home run
9. Waynesboro, Mississippi
10. 15

More Questions About The War-Time Cubs

1. Three and a small part of a fourth
2. Nine
3. 5th
4. #13
5. Eight years in a row
6. 190-189
7. 33
8. Babe Ruth and Jimmy Foxx
9. Philadelphia Athletics
10. Washington College in Chestertown Maryland
11. Philadelphia Phillies
12. 205
13. Eight
14. 'Dim Dom Dal', 'Fire Hydrant', 'Larruping Lilliputian' and 'Tree Stump That Walked Like a Man'
15. 5' 6"
16. Ted Williams
17. Three
18. Paul Erickson
19. Clyde McCullough
20. Catcher

21. He committed four errors in one inning on four successive plays
22. Seven
23. 'The Mad Russian'
24. The Softball Hall of Fame
25. .302
26. 17
27. Puerto Rico
28. 9-14
29. 18-12
30. Seven
31. Harry
32. Center field
33. .292
34. 1942
35. Johnny Vander Meer
36. 6-3
37. 22
38. 32
39. 37
40. Boyceville, Wisconsin
41. Four
42. 314
43. 24
44. 110
45. 36
46. Brooklyn Dodgers
47. 'Deacon'
48. He became a Major League umpire
49. 11-2
50. 36-34

9 - THE TOUGH YEARS

SOME PLAYERS FROM THAT ERA

Bob Rush
1. Battle Creek, Michigan
2. Ransom
3. 110-140

4. Chicago White Sox
5. 127-152

Hank Sauer
1. 'Mayor of Wrigley Field'
2. Peanuts Lowrey and Harry 'The Hat' Walker
3. 198
4. 587
5. Twice
6. Pete Whisenant
7. #9
8. .266
9. 288
10. 876

Ralph Kiner
1. 10
2. $100,000
3. Pitcher Sam Jones and outfielder Gale Wade, plus $60,000
4. 369
5. 1975

More Questions About That Era

1. Cookie Lavagetto
2. When the Cubs rallied for three runs in the bottom of the 9th to win 5-4
3. 135
4. 11-11
5. 18
6. 'Bear Tracks'
7. 18
8. .304
9. 1957
10. Center field
11. Pitcher
12. Shortstop
13. 51
14. 332

15. 21
16. He hit for the cycle
17. 52-70
18. 15-9
19. Five
20. 141-196
21. .325
22. 6' 5"
23. The Cardinals
24. Third base
25. 21
26. Brooklyn Dodgers
27. 88
28. 66
29. 1951
30. .239
31. Two
32. Acting
33. Hit a bases loaded triple
34. .309
35. 184
36. 20
37. Pittsburgh Pirates
38. #14
39. Two games
40. None

10 - THE MAKING OF A SLUGGER

MR. CUB AND TEAMMATE

Ernie Banks
1. Gerry Staley
2. A knuckle ball
3. .275
4. Hit three home runs in a game for the first time
5. Four times
6. Five times
7. Three times
8. September 2, 1965
9. Curt Simmons
10. He hit three triples in one game
11. .274
12. 2,583
13. 1,009
14. 1,636
15. 407
16. 1,305
17. 90
18. Pat Jarvis
19. July 21, 1971
20. August 24, 1971
21. The Reds
22. September 26, 1971
23. A 1st inning single
24. .500
25. 2,528 games

Gene Baker

1. .275
2. Davenport, Iowa
3. Eight
4. 590
5. .265

Other Questions About That Era

1. Pittsburgh
2. Clyde McCullough
3. 4-0
4. Dick Groat, Roberto Clemente, and Frank Thomas
5. Four
6. 185
7. Cardinals
8. 10 home runs
9. 18 to the lead all National League outfielders
10. 23
11. He hit three home runs
12. The Dodgers
13. 26

14. 14-18
15. His jersey got caught in his zipper and he fell off the mound, injuring his left achilles tendon
16. *The Long Season* and *The Pennant Race*
17. Five
18. 32-41
19. $50,000
20. Four
21. Collected his 3,000th career hit
22. Six straight batters
23. Four
24. 15-11
25. 7-11
26. 65
27. 13
28. 10-8
29. He hit for the cycle
30. The Reds
31. .304
32. 24
33. Eight
34. The Dodgers
35. Gene Fodge
36. 1957
37. Catcher
38. Pitcher Don Cardwell and first baseman Ed Bouchee
39. Cincinnati
40. 16-13
41. 10
42. 20
43. Lou Boudreau

11 - THE GREAT EXPERIMENT

A STAR SO BRIGHT, SO SHORT IN LIFE

Ken Hubbs
1. 1959
2. June 13, 1962
3. September 5
4. Cincinnati
5. A throwing error past shortstop Andre Rogers on a double play attempt
6. Dennis Doyle
7. Donn Clendenon of the Pirates
8. Ernie Banks
9. 310
10. .247

More Questions About That Era

1. May 13, 1960
2. He pitched a no-hitter
3. St. Louis Cardinals
4. 4-0
5. 8-14
6. 1959
7. .245
8. 10
9. Hit a home run
10. .303
11. 27 homers
12. 96
13. .318
14. St. Louis
15. Billy Cowan
16. 18
17. Pittsburgh Pirates
18. 5-1
19. 22-10
20. 2.10

21. Hippo Vaughn in 1919
22. Win the Comeback Player-of-the-Year Award
23. From the end of the 1961 season to June 15, 1964
24. .263
25. Hit a 470-foot home run. It was the first ball hit over the green partition into the right center field seats
26. 15-14
27. He had been hitless in 88 at bats
28. 2.55
29. Three seasons
30. He was a submarine ball pitcher

12 - THE LIP AT THE HELM

SOME MEMORABLE MEN OF THAT ERA

Ron Santo
1. Seattle, Washington
2. 23
3. 99
4. 1964
5. 1965
6. Don Young
7. 123
8. August 26, 1972
9. September 21, 1971
10. 28

Billy Williams
1. Rogers Hornsby
2. Tony Taylor
3. Joe Torre of the Milwaukee Braves
4. John Wyatt
5. 1,116
6. September 3, 1970
7. Cleo James
8. To sign a $100,000 contract
9. 426
10. .290

Don Kessinger
1. Forest City, Arkansas
2. University of Mississippi
3. 14
4. August 21, 1971
5. September 22, 1971
6. Pitcher Mike Garman
7. 46-60
8. 1,618
9. 14
10. .252

Glenn Beckert
1. 'Bruno'
2. Allegheny College
3. $8,000
4. 36
5. 27
6. 1971
7. Jerry Morales
8. .283
9. 1,473
10. 243

Ferguson Jenkins
1. Chatham, Ontario
2. .263
3. 21-15
4. 11
5. May 25, 1982
6. San Diego
7. 284
8. 226
9. 3.34
10. 3,192

Chicago Cubs Facts & Trivia

More Questions About That Era

1. 1965
2. Don Drysdale
3. He pitched six shutout innings and won 2-0
4. 9-0
5. He pitched a no-hitter
6. The Atlanta Braves
7. Holtzman pitched his second no-hitter
8. 80-81
9. 20-14
10. 2.49
11. 4-0
12. 92-86
13. San Francisco Giants
14. Pitcher Lindy McDaniel and outfielder Don Landrum
15. 19
16. 149
17. 160
18. 80
19. Center field
20. 10
21. .315
22. 32
23. 115
24. 97
25. The spitball
26. Four
27. Six
28. He pitched a no-hitter against San Diego
29. He came within a pitch of throwing a perfect game. He walked a batter with a full count and two outs in the 9th inning.
30. .307
31. 'Joe Pepitone's Thing'

13 - TOUGH TIMES

SOME PLAYERS OF THAT ERA

Rick Monday
1. He took an American Flag from two men who were trying to burn it
2. It was the 100th anniversary of the Cubs first National League game
3. Three hits
4. 241
5. 106

Bill Madlock
1. The Washington Senators, later to become the Texas Rangers
2. Ron Santo
3. .336
4. Mets pitcher John Matlack
5. Bobby Murcer, Steve Ontiveros, and Andy Muhlstock

Rick Reuschel
1. Camp Point, Illinois
2. In the June 1970 free agent draft
3. San Francisco Giants
4. Hit a pop fly double
5. 1,367

Other Questions About That Era

1. Knuckle-curve
2. Philadelphia Phillies
3. 4-0
4. Seven
5. Los Angeles Dodgers
6. Jim Colborn, Earl Stephenson, and Brock Davis

7. 1973
8. .317
9. 34
10. 1,913
11. 15-10
12. 157-162
13. 82
14. 91
15. 16
16. Four
17. 23-20
18. Pittsburgh Pirates
19. 1976
20. Jim Marshall
21. .298
22. .273
23. 1972
24. Split-finger fastball
25. 1976
26. 2.71
27. 31
28. 1.35
29. 1978
30. 1979
31. 37
32. The Cardinals
33. 238-241
34. .300
35. .324
36. .323
37. 18
38. 201
39. 105
40. Boston Red Sox
41. Shortstop
42. 44
43. Ryne Sandberg and Larry Bowa
44. 27
45. 2½ seasons
46. 38-52
47. 28
48. 48
49. 115
50. New York Mets

14 - CLOSE BUT NO CIGAR: FUTILITY LIVES!

SOME STARS OF THAT ERA

Keith Moreland
1. .302
2. August
3. .333
4. .338
5. 13

Gary Matthews
1. .291
2. 82
3. 103
4. 101
5. 147

Rick Sutcliffe
1. Los Angeles Dodgers
2. 17-10
3. Mel Hall, Joe Carter, Don Schulze, and Darryl Banks
4. June 13, 1987
5. 82-65

Andre Dawson
1. 'Hawk'
2. Montreal Expos
3. 31
4. 104
5. 1987

Mark Grace
1. Eddie Stanky
2. .314
3. 193
4. 46
5. Saddleback College in Mission Viejo, California, and

San Diego State University

Ryne Sandberg
1. .271
2. Twice (1989 & 1990)
3. 245
4. 2,133
5. .289
6. Seven times
7. Twice (1990 & 1991)
8. Five
9. .990
10. One
11. Five years after he retires for good!

More Questions About That Era

1. Philadelphia Phillies
2. After the 1987 season
3. 265-258
4. Four seasons (1982-1985)
5. 23
6. 96
7. Eight seasons (1981-1988)
8. 94
9. 24
10. Eight years (1990-1987)
11. 29
12. 127-158
13. 90
14. 97
15. 25
16. 'The Penguin'
17. Oakland A's
18. April 26, 1985
19. 'Rainbow'
20. .278
21. Center field
22. 27
23. 26
24. 1985
25. 98
26. .296
27. First pick
28. Rafael Palmeiro
29. August 8, 1988
30. Philadelphia Phillies
31. .293
32. Four years (1989-1992)
33. 52
34. 14-6
35. Seven seasons (1986-1992)
36. 36
37. 119
38. Chicago White Sox
39. 131
40. .288
41. 38
42. 53
43. Four home runs
44. Four seasons
45. .303
46. Ed Lynch
47. 7502-7283
48. Philadelphia Phillies
49. Pat Hughes
50. Any answer will do, but hopefully, SOON!

ABOUT THE AUTHOR

Wayne Mausser is the rising new star in sports books. His first work, *Chicago Bears Facts & Trivia*, was completely sold out of book stores within two months of publication, forcing a second printing for the 1995 Christmas season.

Born near "The Field of Dreams" in Iowa, Mausser has spent the past 17 years of his adult life in radio, the last 11 as sports director for several stations. He has hosted numerous football programs involving professional players. He also hosts "Countdown to Kickoff", a one-hour pre-game football show with Ray Scott.

Currently, he works as news and sports director for radio station WPKR in Oshkosh, Wisconsin. He is an avid collector of sports memorabilia, and for recreation, he plays racquetball regularly in the winter and softball in the summer.

READ MORE ABOUT THE CUBS

Over the decades of baseball history, hundreds of books have been written about the Chicago Cubs as a team and as individuals. Jim Enright wrote one of the first histories of the team, and he wrote *Mr. Cub*, the story of Ernie Banks. Cap Anson wrote an autobiography as did Albert Spalding.

In recent years, Art Ahrens and Eddie Gold of Chicago have teamed up to write *Day by Day in Chicago Cubs History*, *The Golden Era Cubs*, and *The New Era Cubs*. Barry Clifford has given us *The Neighborhood of Baseball*, and Larry Names has authored the first volume to his definitive history of the Cubs, *Bury My Heart at Wrigley Field*.

These books and many more about the Cubs and baseball are available at book stores and libraries everywhere, and the author and publisher encourage young readers to check out these books and discover the wonderful past of the Chicago Cubs so that they might better enjoy the present stars and future stars of America's most popular baseball team.

Good reading, everyone!

More interesting and fun-filled books for your reading pleasure!

HEY, WHITE SOX FANS!

Here's the book you've been waiting for!

Chicago White Sox Facts & Trivia
by
Larry Names

History, facts, pictures, and over 1,000 trivia questions and answers about the White Sox!

160 Pages   **ISBN: 0-938313-15-0**

ONLY $9.99

plus shipping, handling, and sales tax

CALL TOLL FREE! AND ORDER NOW!

Call 1-800-993-2665

ATTENTION, BEAR FANS!

Here's the book you've been missing!

CHICAGO BEARS
Facts & Trivia
by
Wayne Mausser

History, facts, pictures, and over 1,000 trivia questions and answers about the Bears!
128 Pages   **ISBN: 0-938313-10-X**

ONLY $7.99
plus shipping, handling, and sales tax

CALL TOLL FREE! AND ORDER NOW!

     Call 1-800-993-2665

HEY, CUB FANS!
Re-live those early days of baseball history in

Bury My Heart at
Wrigley Field

History of the Chicago Cubs: When the Cubs Were the White Sox
by
Larry Names

The most definitive history ever written about the early days of the Chicago Cubs!

HARDCOVER 294 Pages   **ISBN: 0-939995-04-2**

ONLY $20.00
plus shipping, handling, and sales tax

SOFTCOVER 240 Pages   **ISBN: 0-939995-05-0**

ONLY $12.99
Plus shipping, handling, and sales tax

CALL TOLL FREE! AND ORDER NOW!

Call 1-800-993-2665

Any Milwaukee Brewer fans out there? Here's the fun book for you!

Milwaukee Brewers
Facts & Trivia
by
Jeff Everson

History, facts, pictures, and over 1,000 trivia questions and answers about the Brewers!
128 Pages   ISBN: 0-938313-18-8

ONLY $8.99
plus shipping, handling, and sales tax

CALL TOLL FREE! AND ORDER NOW!
Call 1-800-993-2665

Other Great Books for Sports Fans of all Ages!

**History of the Green Bay Packers:
The Lambeau Years, Part I
ONLY $14.95**
plus shipping, handling, and sales tax

**History of the Green Bay Packers:
The Lambeau Years, Part II
ONLY $18.95**
plus shipping, handling, and sales tax

**History of the Green Bay Packers:
The Lambeau Years, Part III
ONLY $18.95**
plus shipping, handling, and sales tax

**History of the Green Bay Packers:
The Shameful Years
ONLY $18.95**
plus shipping, handling, and sales tax

**Green Bay Packers Facts & Trivia
ONLY $12.99**
plus shipping, handling, and sales tax

**Wisconsin Badgers Facts & Trivia
ONLY $4.99**
plus shipping, handling, and sales tax

Milwaukee Bucks Facts & Trivia
ONLY $4.99
plus shipping, handling, and sales tax

St. Louis Rams Facts & Trivia
ONLY $7.99
plus shipping, handling, and sales tax

CALL TOLL FREE! AND ORDER NOW!

Call 1-800-993-2665

AUTOGRAPHS

Wayne Mausser

AUTOGRAPHS